THE MANUAL OF JUDO

THE MANUAL OF JUDO

by

E. J. HARRISON 4th DAN

Author of
" The Fighting Spirit of Japan "
The Art of Jujitsu " " The Art of Wrestling"
&c., &c.

Line Drawings
by R. A. Jackson and the late Dr. H. Shepheard

Foreword
by Kyuzo Mifune 10th Dan of The Kodokan

LONDON
W. FOULSHAM & CO. LTD.
NEW YORK - TORONTO - CAPE TOWN - SYDNEY

W. FOULSHAM & CO. LTD.
Yeovil Road, Slough, Berks., England.

DEDICATION

To my valued Instructor and great friend, the world renowned Judo Master, Kyuzo Mifune, 10th Dan of The Kodokan, Tokyo, Japan, I gratefully dedicate this Manual of Judo, in memory of old times.

ISBN 0 572 01379-5

© *E. J. Harrison 1952*

Printed in Great Britain by
St Edmundsbury Press Ltd, Bury St Edmunds, Suffolk

AUTHOR'S PREFACE

It was, I think, the late Basil Hall Chamberlain, the famous Japanese scholar, who once remarked that it might be regarded as a distinction *not* to have written a book about Japan. Analogously, I am tempted to suggest that in view of the recent rapid expansion of the Judo bibliography in the West, an author innocent of a book on the art seems likely soon to rank as an anomaly. There is thus perhaps a risk inseparable from this class of literary activity of adding " one's sum of more to that which has too much ". Yet the habit once formed cannot easily be eradicated. My own decision to write another book on Judo has been strengthened by my conviction that by no means all the many publications in this domain expound the authentic Kodokan Judo. Moreover, if we are to keep our knowledge of true Judo abreast of developments at the source, then we cannot afford to remain too long passive and non-productive in a literary sense. At the same time I wish to emphasize that I myself disavow any claim to be a Judo " expert ". The implications of that title are far too sweeping to be lightly assumed. Indeed outside Japan there are very few instructors whose combined theoretical and practical knowledge would entitle them to be so considered. On the other hand, were it absolutely essential to restrict printed instruction in Judo to wholly qualified high-ranking Yudansha in Japan, Western aspirants for Judo honours would be condemned to wait perhaps for years before authoritative information became available. Fortunately, however, for the progress of Judo outside Japan, through the intermediary of industrious judoka of lower teaching grades, this important source has been made generally accessible by means of translation and personal contact with the great Japanese Masters, several of whom were my own contemporaries when I practised the art at the Kodokan. I was in fact the first Englishman to be there awarded the initial teaching grade of Shodan or 1st Dan, and today hold the grade of 4th Dan confirmed by the Kodokan. I am also the oldest member of the London Budokwai of which my friend Mr. Gunji Koizumi, 7th Dan, himself the most brilliant exponent of Judo outside Japan, is the founder and present Principal. The Budokwai is directly affiliated to the Tokyo Kodokan and therefore in a position to keep in touch with this fountain-head of technical and theoretical Judo knowledge.

When therefore the reader does me the honour of consulting these pages he may rest assured that the instruction given does not emanate solely from my own brain but has passed, so to speak, through the alembic of far more deeply versed interpreters, and that the methods chosen for description have been subjected to countless empirical tests before their inclusion in the permanent Judo repertoire and curriculum. Furthermore, where necessary I have not hesitated to acknowledge my indebtedness to outside sources for the elaboration of particular fundamental techniques, especially that valuable annual "Kokusai Judo" or "International Judo" issued in Paris under the auspices of the French Federation of Judo. I have similarly taken advantage on occasion of the quarterly Bulletin of the Budokwai for supplementary data on particular methods.

Lastly, I should point out that considering the dynamic nature of the art, compliance with the exacting demands of the Judo purist may later necessitate further amplification and modification of a text which does not pretend to be in any way exhaustive.

The Budokwai,
    15 Lower Grosvenor Place,
        London, S.W.1.

CONTENTS

FOREWORD

Freedom in continuous change! The heart should be
a clear mirror polished a thousand times and should
rely on god-like speed and courage! (signed)
Kyuzo Mifune, 10th Dan, The Kodokan, Tokyo,
March, 1952.

It is a happy chance that the publication of E. J. Harrison's
new book THE MANUAL OF JUDO should almost coincide
with the seventieth anniversary of the foundation of the world-
famous headquarters of Judo, The Kodokan, Tokyo, Japan,
of which he is the oldest living member and where he was
the first Britisher to win the coveted Black Belt during the
Russo-Japanese War of 1904-5. As if in further emphasis of
this auspicious conjuncture, he is the fortunate recipient of a
brief but inspiring message from his old friend and former instructor, Mr. Kyuzo Mifune, 10th Dan, one of the greatest living
exponents of the art and although now verging on seventy still
active and formidable on the mat. A recent photograph of this
renowned Judo Master accompanies the message and is repro-
duced as an illustration of this volume. Above appears a free
translation and facsimile of the original Japanese text.

INTRODUCTORY REMARKS

What is Judo?

THE term Judo today signifies the subtle Japanese art of defence and attack without lethal weapons which, alike in Japan itself and elsewhere in both hemispheres, has largely superseded the older one of Jujutsu (pronounced Jujitsu), also known in feudal days as Taijitsu or Yawara. Judo owes its inception to the genius of the late Dr. Jigoro Kano who, as a very young man eager to develop a neglected physique, studied Jujutsu under many eminent masters of the later feudal times, who were then still living. As he has himself recorded in a book on this subject, although he derived much valuable knowledge from these studies he gradually realized that the instruction given lacked the application of an all-pervading principle, and represented simply the systems of individual schools which were inevitably characterized by many discrepancies and variations in particular methods of throwing, holding, choking and the locking of joints, etc. Dr. Kano's claim to distinction in this sphere may be said to rest upon his conclusion, arrived at through an exhaustive inductive process, that the all-pervading principle should be the highest and most efficient use of both mental and physical energy directed to the accomplishment of a certain definite purpose or aim. Then in the course of careful scrutiny of the numerous techniques he had assimilated from his studies with the old masters, he rejected those that were untenable from this standpoint and substituted new or improved methods fully in harmony with it. The name Judo which he gave to his eclectic system, as eventually elaborated, differs from the older term Jujutsu in that whereas the term Jujutsu is composed of two characters, " ju " meaning " gentle " or " to give way " and " jutsu " meaning " art " or " practice ", in the word Judo the second syllable " do " means a " way " or " principle ".

It is fair to say that one of Dr. Kano's objects was to emphasize this ethical basis of his system which had perhaps been less in evidence among the older ryugi or schools of Jujutsu. For the large-scale teaching of his new system Dr. Kano in 1882 founded the Kodokan in Tokyo. The word literally means a school for studying the way, and in Dr. Kano's exalted mind "the way" meant the concept of life itself.

The success of Kodokan Judo was phenomenal, and ere long its fame as an unrivalled art of defence and attack without arms spread far beyond the confines of Japan, so that today nearly all "civilized" countries possess schools large or small where the art can be studied and practised under reasonably competent instructors.

Rationale of Judo

At the risk of telling some readers facts already known to them and for the benefit of those less well informed. I should explain here that the underlying purpose of Judo is to enable a physically weaker person to defend himself against a physically stronger opponent alike in mimic combat on the mats of the Dojo or exercise hall and in a genuine struggle for survival outside it. Other things equal it is simply axiomatic to say that the stronger man must eventually win, but seeing that not infrequently the relatively poorer physique of one man is largely offset by his superior intelligence, skill and agility, he may conceivably prove the victor in contest with his physically more powerful antagonist. And admitting that there are always numerous gradations of sheer bodily strength among the pupils of any Dojo, the cumulative effect of assiduous study and practice of Judo is bound in the end to convert even a veritable tyro weakling into a physically vigorous and technically skilled Judoka or practitioner of Judo. How often in my own experience as an active student of both Jujutsu and Judo as a young man in Japan have I seen this truth exemplified by the steady transformation during some years of an originally weak Japanese, whom I could easily throw on the mat, into a seasoned yudansha or holder of a Dan (grade, rank, degree) who was capable of turning the tables on me despite my superior natural physique!

I mention these things in order that no young man, however seemingly weak, provided that he is organically sound, need be deterred or discouraged on that score from taking up the study and practice of Judo with the aid of this course, if possible supplemented by the teaching of a competent personal instructor. Will power, tenacity of purpose, coupled with continuous practice not carried to excess can work wonders and are indeed indispensable to the attainment of proficiency in any art or science, and in none more so than in that of Judo.

It should hardly be necessary to remind the student that temperate living, high thinking, the strict observance of bodily hygiene, regular elimination and the sedulous avoidance of sexual excess are part and parcel of the mental, physical and moral equipment of the truly zealous Judoka. Contempt for or neglect of any of these desiderata is calculated to defeat or at any rate retard the end in view.

Essentials for Judo Practice

Under ideal conditions such as exist at the Kodokan, Tokyo, the world headquarters of the art, the floor is covered with quilted mats (tatami) and surrounded with panels of about shoulder height. All nails and pillars with angles have been eliminated to prevent the risk of painful collision. The costume used by the pupil when practising is called judogi and comprises a coat of some strong material capable of resisting constant wear and tear, loose trousers and belt. The last named averages eight or nine feet in length to enable it to be wound twice round the pupil's waist and tied in a double knot in front. Seeing, however, that the present course is designed primarily for those unable to avail themselves of all these facilities, allowance must be made for convenient substitutes and the necessity for improvisation.

Assuming that the neophyte cannot practise regularly at an adequately appointed Dojo or Judo exercise hall, he may have to make shift with a spare room of fair size at home, preferably with a boarded floor upon which perhaps a coconut matting could be laid to soften the shock of falling. The thickly-padded mat used for catch-as-catch-can wrestling is not suitable for Judo because its surface is not smooth enough to permit of the swift and ever changing foot-work essential to the accomplishment of virtually every throw of the copious Judo repertoire. An explanation of the so-called Breakfall which every judoka must master before entering upon actual practice or contest with an opponent will be given later.

The question of costume should not offer any insuperable difficulty. Care should be taken to wear a coat or tunic whose collar and lapels will resist the application of chokelocks or strangleholds without danger of ripping. The loose trousers, preferably of some cotton fabric, should reach well below the knees so as to safeguard these against painful abrasion on the mats. A sash or belt of approximately the prescribed length should be readily available. And here in this connection I must remind the reader that in recognized Dojos affiliated to the Budokwai of London and/or the Kodokan of Tokyo the colour of the belt worn varies according to the grade held by the wearer. The course of Judo is divided into two grades or ranks called respectively " Dan " and " Kyu ". In the Dan grades the numeration ascends from first Dan upwards, whereas in the Kyu grades which precede the Dan grades the numeration descends from 5th Kyu to 1st Kyu which latter immediately precedes the 1st Dan. Further, a white belt is used by all students unqualified for the Dan and Kyu grades and a brown belt by students from the third Kyu up to the first Kyu grade. A black belt is worn by the holders of the five Dan grades; a striped belt of red and white by holders of the sixth up to the ninth Dan grade, and a red belt by holders of the tenth and all higher Dan grades. It may be added that outside Japan the highest Dan so far awarded is the seventh, and even in Japan there are at the time of writing only about three or four tenth Dan instructors.

Thus from what has been said the student will understand that until he has been properly graded by an authorized instructor he ought to wear only a white belt.

Etiquette of Judo

Among Westerners it is customary to shake hands before a boxing or wrestling match. Since Judo owes its origin and evolution to the Japanese, the Japanese method of salutation (*rei wo suru*, in Japanese) has been almost universally adopted among judoka all over the world, and it is always observed both before and after practice and contest. The more ceremonial form is reserved for demonstrations of the Kata and is described as follows by the late Dr. Kano : The contestants squat facing each other with a space of about five feet between them. The insteps should be close to the mat; the hips rest on the heels; the hands are on the mat with the finger-tips turned slightly inward, and when making the bow the back of the head should be as low as the shoulders. However, when practising Randori the salutation may be made with the toes and hips raised a little, but the movements of hands and head must always be formal, as previously described. At the Kodokan and other Judo schools in Japan, such salutations are not confined to the actual contestants on the mat but are made by the pupil in the direction of the dais or platform on which superiors and instructors may be seated, both when he enters and leaves the Dojo or Judo exercise hall. However, in Judo schools in the West the accepted etiquette is hardly so strict, but the foregoing form of salutation is never omitted between judoka in practice and contest.

Divisions of Judo

I am anxious not to confuse the student at the outset with too much detail and so for the moment shall confine myself to a general classification of the principal branches of the art which can later be elaborated if and when he wishes to progress to a more advanced stage of proficiency. Here then we have the relevant divisions designated in English with their Japanese equivalents.

The Art of Throwing (Nagewaza) comprising :
   Art of Throwing in a Standing Position (Tachiwaza) and
   Art of Throwing in a Lying Position (Sutemiwaza).

These main divisions are further sub-divided into :
   Hand Technique (Tewaza)
   Loin, Waist or Hip Technique (Koshiwaza) and
   Foot and Leg Technique (Ashiwaza).

The Art of Throwing in a Lying Position is sub-divided into :
   Throwing with one's back on the ground (Masutemiwaza) and

   Throwing with one's side on the ground (Yokosutemiwaza).

The Art of Clinching (Katamewaza, literally " hardening " or " defence ") comprising :

   Art of Holding (Osaekomiwaza)
   Art of Choking (Shimewaza or Shiboriwaza) and
   Art of Bending and Twisting the Joints (Kansetsuwaza)

An overall term for this division is Groundwork or Newaza. The third and last division of Judo is the Art of Attacking Vital Spots (Atemiwaza or Atewaza) with arms, bands, elbows, fingers, by means of thrusting, poking, striking, kicking, etc. This branch of Judo is taught only to students that have attained the Dan or Black Belt grade and need not therefore be dwelt upon at this initial stage of the tyro's training.

The same remark applies to the esoteric art of resuscitation called Katsu and Kappo which is taught also only to Dan holders.

The first two main divisions of Judo are as a rule practised in three ways, viz., in free exercise called Randori, forms demonstrated in a prearranged sequence called Kata, and in actual contest called Shobu or Shiai, but for the purpose of this course it will suffice to explain the various tricks or techniques in their Randori and/or Shobu exemplification as calculated to prove most useful in an emergency.

None the less it is perhaps worth while adding the several kinds of Kata or Forms generally taught today at the Tokyo Kodokan. These comprise seven classes in all, viz., (1) Forms of Throwing or Nage-no-Kata; (2) Forms of Grappling or better Clinching, otherwise Groundwork or Katame-no-Kata; (3) Forms of so-called Gentleness; (4) Forms of Decision; (5) Forms Antique; (6) Forms of "Five"; and (7) Forms of National Physical Education, based on the principle of Maximum-Efficiency. The Forms of Throwing are devised for the study of theory and practice of all the techniques of throwing and clinching (groundwork) generally used in Free Exercise or Randori. The so-called Forms of Gentleness are very gentle movements designed to train the pupil in the management of the body in attack and defence, and how to employ one's strength most effectively. The Forms of Decision aim at the teaching of the principle of body management and the theory of attack and defence coupled with the methods of attacking vital spots (Kyusho). The so-called Forms Antique and those of "Five" teach the general principle underlying the relevant techniques and include many interesting phases of Judo. The Forms of National Physical Education (based on the principle of Maximum-Efficiency) are virtually group exercises. Some of the movements are taken from the Forms of Gentleness and Decision. As far as I know, a complete repertoire of these Forms has not yet been publicly demonstrated in this country. A list of the throws included in the Nage-no-Kata, most frequently demonstrated in public displays of Judo, will be found in the attached glossary.

Importance of deep abdominal breathing

In my book entitled " The Fighting Spirit of Japan," published a good many years ago by the late T. Fisher Unwin, I was the first to reveal to the Western world the esoteric element which enters into nearly all Japanese arts and crafts but in none more so perhaps than in the so-called Martial Arts (Bujutsu) among which Jujutsu and today Judo may be included. The subject in its entirety lies beyond the scope of the present course but the particular branch that treats of deep abdominal breathing as an indispensable aid to the highest proficiency is of such vital importance to all aspiring judoka that I offer no apology for devoting a section of these pages to a comparatively brief explanation of the method advocated by recognized experts for the attainment of the most satisfactory results under this head.

The purpose of this method of deep abdominal breathing is to develop the *saika tanden* or lower abdominal region to which Japanese fighting men attach more importance than to the chest, in contradistinction to the usual Western practice. One of the simplest methods of developing this region is described as follows : Take a piece of cotton cloth about six feet long, fold it twice and pass it twice round the stomach just below the lower ribs, and fasten it tightly in that position. Then try to inhale the air through your nose deep down into your stomach. Repeat the process three or four hundred times a day or even two or three thousand times if you can get used to it ! In so doing keep your body soft, hold your shoulders well drawn down, your back bent forward, and sit or squat in such a manner that the tip of your nose hangs over your navel. Accustom yourself when sitting to press your seat with your hips as it were, and when walking to project your abdomen beyond your feet. These directions may be difficult to fulfil literally, but the idea is to regulate your movements as if you had the above-mentioned object always in view. When facing an opponent, whether in a standing or a sitting posture, look him steadfastly in the face but do not omit even for a moment to have your mind's eye directed to your *saika tanden,* i.e., take care to breathe as already instructed and in this way you will not be disturbed by foreign objects.

This practice of deep abdominal breathing has from time immemorial in Japan been closely associated with the cultivation of what is called the Kiai (literally "spirit-meeting", pro-

nounced "kee-eye"), an occult shout supposed to emanate
from the region of the lower abdomen or *saika tanden* and
credited with the power of reducing an inferior antagonist to
helplessness and so placing him at the mercy of the other. And
next to deep breathing, the most essential physical condition of
the art of the Kiai is the regulation of one's posture. The first
desideratum is to keep the body soft, pliant and elastic, like
rubber. To achieve this condition, again, it is necessary to
concentrate one's vigour in the *saika tanden* while keeping one's
chest empty. The posture has an important bearing upon the
breathing and the two must be studied concurrently. The
second point to be observed is to keep the mouth closed and
the chin well drawn in towards the throat. Try to keep the
ears in a line with the shoulders and the nose on a line with the
navel. If you keep your mouth shut and your chin drawn back,
the principal muscles of the throat are made taut and the
spinal column is strengthened. The latter in turn imparts
proper vigour to the lower abdomen. Some authorities favour
exhalation through the clenched teeth after every inhalation
deep down into the lower abdomen, but perhaps the consensus
of opinion would favour exhalation through the nose. The
latter has always been my own practice.

In this connection I must at the very outset impress upon the
pupil that in the execution of every throw, hold and lock
described in the present course, it is not sufficient to confine
the movement to the arms and legs; on the contrary, in all
cases he must try to bring into play the force emanating from
the lower abdomen or *saika tanden*, also more colloquially
called the *shitahara*. Other things being equal, the judoka
with the better developed *saika tanden*, the result of systematic
deep breathing as already described, is almost certain to beat
an adversary his inferior in this respect.

Signals of Defeat. Unless these are well understood from
the outset, painful and even dangerous consequences may easily
ensue in both practice and contest, more particularly when
chokelocks and bonelocks are being applied. In most Judo
schools the defeated contestant taps his victor's jacket several
times in the nearest accessible spot, whereupon the victor must
at once relax his hold. In Japan, if the victim has not been
deprived of the power of speech, he generally exclaims
"Maitta!" ("I'm beaten!").

GLOSSARY

OWING to their greater conciseness and brevity in comparison
with their English equivalents, the Japanese terms descriptive
of the numerous methods and techniques of the art of Judo
tend to be constantly more and more used by non-Japanese
judoka (students of Judo) in Europe and America. The
appended nomenclature does not include anything like an
exhaustive list of the many throws and holds described elsewhere in the text, but does provide a fairly comprehensive
selection of the respective categories pertaining to such techniques together with a number of terms belonging to the
esoteric branch of the art which should properly be studied
by more advanced judoka interested in its underlying
philosophy and rationale.

Hints on pronunciation: No useful purpose would be
served by my attempting to include in this section guidance on
pronunciation of the Japanese terminology comprehensive
enough to meet every contingency. Judoka wishing to extend
their knowledge under this head will be well advised to con-
sult a good Japanese grammar or better still, if possible, seek
out a Japanese teacher and learn the correct sounds from him
by ear. Here I must content myself with a few general rules
observance of which should enable the judoka to pronounce
the appended terms well enough to make himself understood
by any intelligent Japanese listener.

There are long and short vowels in Japanese. Although the
description is not strictly accurate, yet for most practical purposes the judoka may safely pronounce the vowels as in the
Latin languages. It is, however, important to make a clear
distinction between the long and short *o* and *u*. Thus in such
terms as " Ogoshi," " Osotogari," " Osoto-otoshi," etc., the
initial *o*, meaning " large " or " great," should be pronounced
as a long vowel and in recognized grammars is always printed
with a diacritical stroke above it. For greater convenience of

23

printing this stroke has been omitted in the following pages. The short vowel *u* sounds like *u* in the word *rude*. The vowel *e* is never silent and sounds much as *e* in *pen*. On the other hand, both *i* and *u* are frequently almost mute and therefore quite unaccented. Where necessary this distinction is shown in the appended glossary.

Among consonants special attention should be paid to the *g*. In the body of the word and in the particle *ga* it has the sound of *ng* in *king*. At the beginning of a word and in words formed by reduplication, with which latter the judoka need not concern himself, it has the hard sound of *g* in *goat*. Thus according to the former rules the term Hanegoshi is pronounced as though written "Hanehngoshi," Haraigoshi as though written "Haraingoshi," Ogoshi as though written "Ohngoshi," Migi as though written "Mingi." etc. The frequently recurring diphthong *ai* sounds like *ai* in *aisle, ei* approximately like *eh*. In the so-called Tokyo dialect, nowadays spoken by all educated Japanese, an initial *h* when succeeded by the vowel *i* tends to sound like *sh*, e.g., the term "Hidari-shizentai" (Left Natural Posture) is often pronounced as though written "Shidari-shizentai," but not quite so strongly.

Aite :	Opponent, adversary.
Ashi-ate :	Art of attacking vital spots with the foot.
Ashiwaza :	Foot and leg technique.
Atewaza : Atemiwaza or	Art of attacking vital spots in the body.
Awasewaza :	Combination throws.
Ayumi-ashi :	Ordinary step.
Bu :	Military (martial) affairs.
Bujutsu :	Martial arts.
Butsukari :	Method of practising throws up to the point of breaking opponent's balance without actually throwing him.
Chikara :	Strength.
Chugaeri :	Forward somersault used in Breakfall.

| Dan : | Grade or degree indicated by wearing of Black Belt. Thus : |

Shodan means 1st Dan
Nidan   „   2nd Dan
Sandan   „   3rd Dan
Yodan   „   4th Dan
Godan   „   5th Dan
Rokudan   „   6th Dan
Shichidan „   7th Dan
Hachidan „   8th Dan
Kudan   „   9th Dan
Judan   „   10th Dan

Do :	The trunk, e.g., Dojime—Trunk Squeezing.
Dojo :	Judo exercise hall.
Eri :	Neck band or lapel.
Fudoshin :	Imperturbability of mind in emergency.
Fukushiki-kokyu :	Deep abdominal breathing.
Fumi-komi :	Stepping in.
Fusegi :	Defence.
Genki :	Vigour, energy, vitality.
Gonosen-no-Kata :	Prearranged demonstration of throws and counter throws.
Gyaku :	Reverse, adverse, applied to methods of choking and holding, e.g., Gyakuju-jijime—Reverse Necklock or Chokelock.
Hadaka :	Naked, e.g., Hadakajime—Naked Chokelock.
Hantei :	Decision.
Hara :	Stomach, abdomen, e.g., Shita-hara —lower abdomen.
Harai :	Sweep, e.g., Haraigoshi—Sweeping Loin.
Hasami :	Scissors.
Hen-O :	Adaptation to the situation.

Hidari :   Left.

Hidari-shizentai :   Left Natural Posture.

Hiji :   Elbow, e.g., Hiji-ate—Attacking vital spots with the elbow.

Hikiwake :   Drawn match.

Hishigi :   Crush, break, etc., e.g., Ashihishigi— Leg Crush.

Hiza :   Knee, e.g., Hizaguruma — Knee Wheel.

Hizagashira-ate :   Attacking vital spots with the knee-cap.

Ippon :   One point (for a throw, etc. in contest).

Jigotai :   Self-defensive Posture.

Jozu na :   Skilful, adroit. The *o* is a long vowel.

Judogi :   Judo costume.

Judoka :   Person practising Judo.

Jutsu (Jitsu) :   Art, as in Jujutsu—Soft Art.

Juji :   Cross, e.g., Namijuji—Normal Cross Chokelock.

Jukuren :   Skill, dexterity, etc.

Ju-no-Kata :   Slow motion demonstration of basic principles.

Kaeshiwaza :   Counter technique.

Kake :   Act of throwing, attack.

Kangeiko :   Midwinter Judo practice.

Kansetsuwaza :   Art of bending and twisting the joints.

Kappo :   System of resuscitation.

Kata :   Formal system of prearranged exercises in attack and defence. When written with another character the word means "shoulder", e.g., "Kataguruma" —Shoulder Wheel. There are fifteen throws illustrated in the Kata or Forms and for purposes of reference they are specified below with both their original

Japanese and English names. Since each throw can be applied from either side, their sum-total is properly thirty, but as a rule, when publicly demonstrated, the Torite or Taker confines himself to applying them from one side only, i.e., the right natural or right self-defensive posture (migishizentai and migijigotai).

Japanese name	*English name*
Ukiotoshi	Floating Drop
Seoinage	Shoulder Throw
Kataguruma	Shoulder Wheel
Ukigoshi	Floating Loin or Waist
Haraigoshi	Sweeping Loin
Tsurikomigoshi	Lift-pull Loin
Ashiharai	Foot Dash or Sweep
Tsurikomiashi	Drawing Ankle Throw
Uchimata	Inner Thigh
Tomoenage	Stomach Throw
Uranage	Rear Throw
Sumigaeshi	Corner Throw
Yokogake	Side Body Drop
Yokoguruma	Side or Lateral Wheel
Ukiwaza	Floating Throw

All the foregoing throws are described in their proper context in this manual.

Katame-no-Kata :   Prearranged Forms of Groundwork comprising hold-downs or immobilization methods, necklocks, and methods of bending and twisting the joints.

Katamewaza :   Technique of clinching or immobilization. Groundwork.

Katsu :   System of resuscitation.

Keiko :   Practice as opposed to contest.

Keikogi :   Practice costume.

Kesa :   Scarf, e.g., Kesagatame—Scarf Hold, one of the methods of immobilization in Groundwork.

Kiai (pronounced "Kee-eye") :   Occult shout supposed to emanate from the lower abdomen (saika tanden or shitahara).

Kime-no-Kata :   Prearranged methods or forms of defence and attack.

Ko :   Small, minor, e.g., Kosotogari—Minor Exterior Reaping.

Kobushi-ate :   Attacking vital spots with the fist.

Kodokan :   Judo Headquarters in Tokyo.

Koshiwaza :   Loin or waist technique.

Kubi :   Neck, e.g., Kubigatame—Necklock.

Kumi :   Grapple with.

Kumi-kata :   Methods of taking hold of opponent's lapel or belt, etc.

Kuzure :   Break down, e.g., Kuzurekamishiho-gatame—Broken Upper Four Quarters.

Kuzushi :   Disturbing opponent's posture or balance. There are eight of these, viz.,
(1) Front Kuzushi (Mamae-no-Kuzushi)
(2) Back Kuzushi (Maushiro-no-Kuzushi)
(3) Left Kuzushi (Hidari-mayoko-no-Kuzushi)
(4) Right Kuzushi (Migi-mayoko-no-Kuzushi)
(5) Right front corner Kuzushi (Migi-maesumi-no-Kuzushi)
(6) Left front corner Kuzushi (Hidari-maesumi-no-Kuzushi)
(7) Right back corner Kuzushi (Migi-ushirosumi-no-Kuzushi)
(8) Left back corner Kuzushi (Hidari-ushirosumi-no-Kuzushi).

Kwai or Kai :   Society, club.

Kwansetsu or Kansetsu :   Joint. Hence : Kansetsuwaza or art of bending and twisting the joints.

Kyu :   Class, grade, rank, e.g.,
Rokkyu means 6th class
Gokyu   „   5th class
Shikyu   „   4th class
Sankyu   „   3rd class
Nikyu   „   2nd class
Ikkyu   „   1st class

Kyusho :	Vital spot in the body.
Ma :	An emphatic prefix, e.g., Masutemi-waza—Throwing in direct lying position.
Maitta :	Exclamation " I'm beaten!"
Maki-komi :	Roll in, e.g., Sotomakikomi—Outer winding throw.
Mata :	Thigh, e.g., Uchimata—Inner Thigh Throw.
Migi :	Right.
Migishizentai :	Right natural posture.
Mitchaku suru :	To establish contact.
Mochi :	Hold with the hands.
Mokuso or Mokko :	Meditation, contemplation, reverie.
Montei :	Disciple or pupil.
Morote :	Both hands, e.g., Morote Seoinage—Shoulder Throw with both hands.
Mudansha :	Judo pupil below Black Belt grade. The prefix " mu " signifies negation, " nothing ", " nil ", etc., i.e., " Nil Dan Holder ".
Mune :	Breast.
Muri :	Unreasonable, commonly applied to incorrect use of force when attempting a throw.
Nage-no-Kata :	Prearranged forms of throwing.
Nesshin :	Zeal, enthusiasm, fervour, etc.
Newaza :	Groundwork.
Nigiri-katami :	Closing fingers firmly with the thumbs bent underneath, a method supposed to impart resolution and courage to the subject.
Nyumon suru :	To become a pupil, join the Dojo.
O :	Big, great. The o is a long vowel. Hence : Osotogari — Major Exterior Reaping.

Obi :   Belt, sash, e.g., Obiotoshi—Belt Drop.

Osaekomiwaza :   Art of holding, immobilizing opponent on the ground.

Randori :   Free exercise.

Rei wo suru :   To make salutation.

Renzokuwaza :   Successive technique.

Ryugi :   School, system. The *u* is a long vowel.

Saika tanden :   Lower abdomen.

Sasae :   Support, e.g., Sasae-Tsurikomi-Ashi —Propping Drawing Ankle Throw.

Sasoku :   Left side.

Sensei :   Teacher.

Seoi :   Carry on the shoulder, hence : Seoinage—Shoulder Throw.

Shiai :   Contest.

Shibori :   Strangle, choke, e.g., Shiboriwaza— Technique of choking or strangling.

Shihan :   Teacher, instructor.

Shiho :   Four directions, e.g., Kamishihogatame—Locking of Upper Four Quarters.

Shimewaza :   Art of choking.

Shintai :   "Advance or Retreat"—foot movement in Judo. Written with another character it also means " body ".

Shisei :   Posture.

Shizenhontai :   Fundamental natural posture.

Shizentai :   Natural posture.

Shitahara :   Lower abdomen. The *i* is mute, i.e., " Shtahara ".

Shobu :   Contest.

Shochugeiko :   Midsummer Judo practice.

Sode :   Sleeve, e.g., Sodeguruma — Sleeve Wheel—method of choking.

Sumi :   Corner, e.g., Sumi-gaeshi—Corner Throw.

Sutemiwaza :	Art of throwing in a lying position. The word " sutemi " means literally " self-abandonment ". It is pronounced " stemi ".
Tachiwaza :	Art of throwing in a standing position.
Tai :	Body. Hence : Tai-otoshi — Body Drop.
Tai-Sabaki :	Turning movement.
Tanden :	Abdomen.
Tatami :	Mat.
Te :	Hand, also trick.
Tewaza :	Hand technique.
Tekubi :	Wrist.
Tokui :	Pet throw.
Torite :	" Taker " (the partner that effects the throw) in Kata or prearranged forms.
Tsugiashi :	Following foot, method of foot movement in Judo.
Tsukuri :	Destroying balance or fitting action for attack (Kake). The first u is almost mute, i.e. " Tskuri ".
Tsurikomi :	Lift-pull on opponent's collar and sleeve.
Tsuyoi :	Strong, powerful.
Uchi :	Interior. Hence : Uchi-mata—Inner Thigh throw.
Ude :	Arm. Hence : Ude-garami — Entangled Arm Lock in Kansetsuwaza.
Ude-ate :	Art of attacking the vital spots with the arm.
Ukemi :	Method of falling in Breakfall. Literally : " Falling Way ".
Ukete :	" Receiver " in Kata or prearranged forms of attack and defence.
Uku :	To float, e.g., Ukiwaza—Floating Throw.

Ura :   Opposite, reverse, obverse, etc., e.g., Uranage—Rear Throw.

Waza :   Trick, skill, technique.

Yama :   Mountain. Hence : Yama-arashi— Mountain Storm throw.

Yawara :   Old name of Jujutsu.

Yoko :   Side. Hence : Yokoguruma — Side Wheel Throw.

Yudansha :   Holder of the Dan Grade (Black Belt) in Judo.

INSTRUCTION I

ART OF THROWING FROM A STANDING POSITION (TACHIWAZA)
—RELEVANT POSTURES—BREAKING OF POSTURE OR BALANCE
(KUZUSHI)—MOVEMENT—TSUKURI AND KAKE—TAI-SABAKI
THE BREAKFALL—BUTSUKARI—KUMI-KATA—FUSEGI AND
KAESHIWAZA—CONTACT

IT goes without saying that in order to achieve the most satisfactory results it is most advisable that at the very beginning
of your studies under this course you should enlist the co-
operation of a like-minded partner.

It will be clear that Judo differs from, say, weight-lifting and
various other purely physical culture systems which can be
practised solo, and that like wrestling, boxing and fencing it
requires a living opponent with whom to practise. True, a few
of the essential preliminary movements can be acquired alone,
but after that stage in your progress you simply cannot dispense
with a congenial companion equally interested in the art.

My first lesson in that branch of Judo concerned with
throwing an opponent from the standing position deals with the
assumption of a correct posture, methods of breaking your
opponent's posture, otherwise his balance, and mastery of
what is called the Breakfall. The last-named factor is indispensable in actual practice or contest because unless you know
how to fall properly you run the risk of more or less serious
injury from clumsy impact against the mat.

Now before undertaking any of the throws which I intend
to describe in my next instruction, you should take careful note
of and try to reproduce the following six postures in their
stated sequence, viz. : —

1. *Fundamental Natural Posture (Shizenhontai)*. In this
you stand as shown in the accompanying Fig. 1, quite naturally
with your feet about 12 inches apart and your arms held
loosely at your sides. From this fundamental natural posture
stem out :

Right Natural Posture (Migishizentai) in which you stand
with your right hand outstretched and your right foot

33

Fig. 1

Fig. 2

Fig. 3

Fig. 4

advanced. If confronting an opponent you lightly grasp his left lapel with your right hand and his right sleeve at the elbow with your left hand (Fig. 2).

Left Natural Posture (Hidarishizentai) in which you stand with your left foot and hand advanced, and if confronting an opponent, you lightly grasp his right lapel with your left hand and his left sleeve at the elbow with your right hand.

As a modification of these three natural postures, arising from the exigencies of free practice (Randori) or contest (Shobu or Shiai) Judo also recognizes :

Fundamental Self-defensive Posture (Jigohontai) in which you stand with your legs farther apart than in the Fundamental Natural Posture, approximately one step instead of one foot, and with the waist slightly lowered, as shown in Fig. 3.

Right Self-defensive Posture (Migijigotai) in which, as in the case of the Right Natural Posture, you stand with right foot and arm advanced, but, in contradistinction to the latter, with both legs bent (Fig. 4).

Left Self-defensive Posture (Hidarijigotai) in which you stand with your left arm and foot advanced, but with legs bent. The relative holds on your opponent's lapel and elbow are exactly the same as in the natural postures. The two divisions may be summed up as below :

Natural Postures $\begin{cases} \text{Fundamental Natural Posture} \\ \text{Right Natural Posture} \\ \text{Left Natural Posture} \end{cases}$

Self-defensive Postures $\begin{cases} \text{Fundamental Self-defensive Posture} \\ \text{Right Self-defensive Posture} \\ \text{Left Self-defensive Posture} \end{cases}$

Breaking or disturbing balance or posture (Kuzushi)

For the purpose of disturbing an opponent's balance or, in Judo terminology, breaking his posture in order to render him vulnerable to a contemplated throw in Randori (free practice) or Shobu or Shiai (contest), eight ways of so-called Kuzushi, derived from the Japanese verb *kuzusu* meaning to break, change, simplify, etc., and based on the fundamental natural posture, have been elaborated. They are (1) Front Kuzushi (Mamae-no-Kuzushi); (2) Back Kuzushi (Maushiro-no-Kuzushi); (3) Left Kuzushi (Hidari-mayoko-no-Kuzushi); (4) Right Kuzushi (Migi-mayoko-no-Kuzushi); (5) Right front corner Kuzushi (Migimae-sumi-no-Kuzushi); (6) Left front

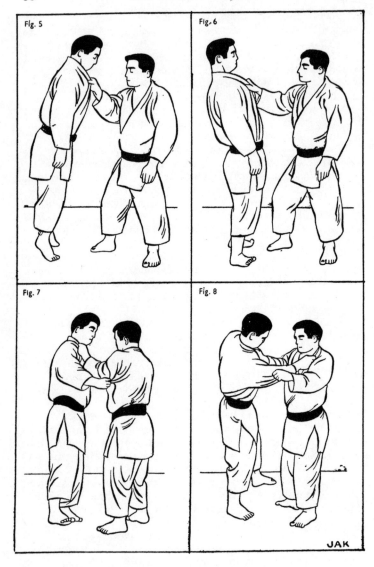

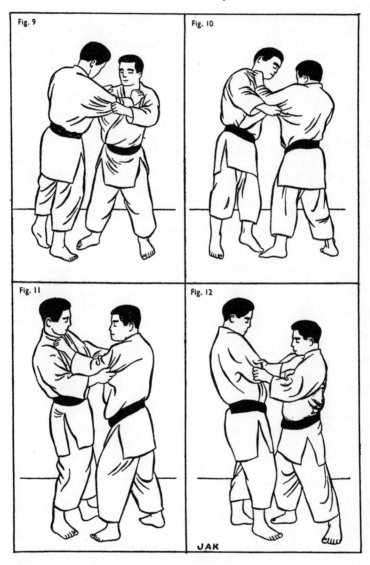

Fig. 9

Fig. 10

Fig. 11

Fig. 12

JAK

corner Kuzushi (Hidarimae-sumi-no-Kuzushi); (7) Right back corner Kuzushi (Migiushiro-sumi-no-Kuzushi) and (8) Left back corner Kuzushi (Hidariushiro-sumi-no-Kuzushi). Please note carefully these eight different ways in the accompanying figures (Figs. 5-12). I ought to add that in actual practice the left Kuzushi (3) and right Kuzushi (4) are rarely conclusive; more often than not they tend almost immediately to be transformed into a left front or back corner Kuzushi or right front or back corner Kuzushi, as the case may be, in which posture it is generally easier for the assailant to press home his attack. Do not forget that in whatever direction you are trying to disturb your opponent's posture, it is essential that the dynamic impulse should not be confined to your arms and legs alone but must be, as it were, reinforced by the centrifugal force emanating from your lower abdomen or *saika tanden*. See the paragraph in my introductory remarks on deep abdominal breathing. Also in applying Kuzushi be careful not to raise your elbows without immediate action, since in that position you expose yourself to dangerous counter-attack.

In connection with what has been said above, I cannot do better than quote some remarks made by Mifune, 10th Dan and the late Hashimoto, 9th Dan of the Kodokan, on the execution of throws : " It is necessary for you to realize the importance of full use of the body mechanism, from your little finger to your big toe. In this way vour power comes from the use of your weight, your abdominal muscles and your shoulders. You must not use your arms or legs locally but your whole body as a unit, getting your results from the Tanden (abdomen). For these results it may be as well to remind you of the importance of applying forces *longitudinally*. When pushing against something with a stick, it is very difficult to get any useful result by a lateral movement, but by a thrust along the length of the stick all your strength can be brought into play. In Judo this principle applies to all use of the wrists, arms and body."

Movement (Shintai, literally " advance or retreat ")

Mastery of correct movement is all important in Judo. Be careful when advancing or retreating, when turning to right or left, to rest the weight of your body on the so-called leading foot. In actual practice or contest the accepted method of movement, which in time becomes virtually automatic, is for one foot to be used as the leading foot, while your other trailing foot comes up to within a few inches of the leading foot before the next step is taken. On no account should your feet be brought very close together or crossed, and be careful to bring up your trailing foot not too close to your leading foot before your leading foot has taken the next step. Neglect of these precautions will imperil your balance. In Judo terminology this foot technique is called " Tsugiashi " meaning literally " next " or " following foot."

Another important point to be observed is that in movement the feet should be very little if at all raised from the mat, but preferably slid in a manner somewhat reminiscent of-the dance chassé.

And in connection with this important subject of movement, please make a careful note of the following basic principle : When engaged in Randori or free practice, and your opponent tries to push you, do not push back against him; instead you should move backwards and try to pull him slightly more than he is pushing you but without losing your own balance. Similarly if your opponent is pulling you, contrive to advance against him a thought more rapidly than he is pulling you but without losing your balance. Observance of this principle will facilitate your aim to break your opponent's posture or balance and thus expose him to your effective attack.

In the same context it should be self-evident that even when engaged with an opponent of approximately equal physical strength, you cannot hope to throw him unless and until you have broken his posture or balance in one or other of the above mentioned directions. And if he happens to be physically stronger than yourself, adherence to the correct technique becomes even more important. It would, for example, be a waste of energy to try to throw him if he had one foot or both feet firmly planted on the ground. The ideal moment for an attempted throw is a split second before his leading foot is firmly planted or if you have his posture so broken that he is tilted forward on the toes of that foot. This rule is equally valid whether your opponent's posture has been broken towards his right or left front corner or towards his direct front, when either foot might be vulnerable to attack, or when your opponent's posture is broken towards his right or left *back* corner or direct back and he is canted backwards on his heel or heels, although your chosen throw will necessarily be determined by the particular direction in which you have broken his posture, and will vary accordingly. Throws pertinent to these changing conditions will be described in their proper place.

The leg that is not advancing, i.e., on which your opponent is not resting, is in Japanese Judo parlance sometimes called the " floating " leg, and it is rarely advisable to attack that leg since the retention of his balance does not depend upon it to the same extent as upon the leading leg or foot.

Do not get discouraged if in the early stages of your novitiate you cannot successfully translate these basic principles into practice. And indeed reflect that when you are sufficiently skilful to do so, say, more often than not in practice or contest, with an opponent one degree below the Dan grade, you will already have qualified for the coveted Black Belt. Dogged patience and perseverance are just as important and necessary ingredients of your mental and moral make-up as are good health and strength of your purely physical equipment, for success in your study of this fascinating art. And the primary object of countless repetitions of your chosen throws is to render your response to your opponent's every move virtually a reflex action.

One other principle should be noted : Unless in the very act of applying a throw, hold or lock, avoid tension and rigidity when grasping your opponent's lapel and sleeve in any of the natural or self-defensive postures already described. To adopt a simile used by my renowned teacher Sakujiro Yokoyama, your arms should serve as chains loosely connecting you with your antagonist or as an electric cable along which his impulses and contemplated moves may be conveyed to you at the moment of their inception. On the other hand, if you persist in keeping a strong grip on your opponent's lapel and your arms stiff, you will not only all the sooner tire yourself but owing to the cultivation of this bad habit, when you come to apply a throw, both your Tsukuri and Kake will lack the speed and suppleness essential to their success. This bad habit will also deprive your contemplated attack of the element of surprise which in its turn is indispensable to the successful execution of every Judo technique.

If you are always afraid of being thrown, especially in Randori, and although perhaps you may, if ever on the defensive, prove a difficult man to throw, you can never hope by such tactics to develop into an efficient Judoka with ability to throw the other fellow. In the early stages of your training it is almost

inevitable that the bold essay of any new throw will expose
you to the risk of a counter. Yet if you are wise you will make
light of this risk and always go "full out" for every throw
regardless of the consequences. Once you are satisfied that you
have detected a good opening, do not resist the impulse to
attack, or in boxing parlance, do not pull your punches.

Tsukuri and Kake (pronounced "Kah-kay")

Literally the Japanese word Tsukuri means "make," "con-
struction," "workmanship," while Kake means "beginning"
or "start," but in their Judo connection they have a special
technical significance.

Thus Tsukuri is the power of destroying your opponent's
posture or balance described above. It is an indispensable
preliminary to the decisive application of the particular technique you have in mind for your opponent's overthrow. Then
the instant you are satisfied that you have broken his posture
or balance in the required direction, go all out for the relevant
throw.

The movement synchronizing with the application of the
required technique is known as Kake or, as one might say, the
attack itself, i.e., the actual throw. When demonstrated by an
expert the transition from Tsukuri to Kake may be so swift and
subtle as to elude detection by an inexperienced onlooker.
Faulty Tsukuri can very easily spoil your Kake, even though
the latter has intrinsically been correctly applied. And
admittedly an exceptionally powerful Judoka may succeed in
throwing his opponent despite incorrect Tsukuri and Kake
because of the use of brute strength, but he is none the less
violating the basic principles of the art and unless he corrects
this fault in good time, he can hardly expect to develop into a
really skilful exponent of Judo. Japanese instructors at the
Kodokan are never impressed by such exhibitions of mere
"beef," and even if the contestant guilty thereof scores a
victory, they usually dismiss it contemptuously as "muri" or
"unreasonable."

Tai-Sabaki

A third important factor in the throwing process is called
Tai-Sabaki. The word is composed of two characters, the first
"Tai" meaning "body" and the second "Sabaki" meaning
literally "management" or "judgment," but in Judo context
the expression may be freely rendered as the turning move-

ment or action of the body which must by a split second precede the throw. Here I shall quote with grateful acknowledgment from the valuable French " Judo International" (Kokusai Judo) published under the patronage of the French Federation of Judo, part of an explanation of this all-important principle given by the late Honda, 9th Dan of the Kodokan, as follows : " In an overhead view, the line of the hips and shoulders may be likened to a bar turning about its centre of gravity. If pushed at one of its ends it will turn, and the only way to overturn it is a push exactly at the centre of gravity 'A'. If we suppose, however, that the bar is free to move and that its centre can take up any desired position not only at the middle but at either end, then by placing 'A' outside the line of the thrust its weakness is changed into strength. This is so for the human body. In Judo, to give the maximum leverage the turning axis for any throw is almost always at the end of the bar, that is, about a shoulder or hip. For example, in such throws as Seoinage (Shoulder Throw), Ogoshi (Major Hip or Major Loin Throw), Tai-otoshi (Body Drop), etc., when they are executed to the right, i.e., towards your opponent's right-hand side, you must turn to the left on the toes of your right foot, using the right hip or shoulder as axis or fulcrum. In this way the left hand and shoulder are used to the utmost advantage in the throw. If, on the other hand, you turn your body as if it were pivoted at the centre about a vertical axis, the arm of the lever is much shorter and the resulting movement in a circle will not break the opponent's balance to advantage. If Tai-Sabaki is well done, the opponent's hand on the inside of the turn should not hinder you." In general, Tai-Sabaki may be described as a balancing movement for the body and should be practised daily as part of your training. Our efforts must be so directed that the body will be capable of light movement in any direction whatsoever.

The Breakfall

Before you can safely engage in Randori with a living partner you must thoroughly master the knack of falling in such a manner as to avoid shock or injury from violent impact against the mat. The Japanese expressions of " Ukemi " or " falling-way," more literally " being acted upon," " defensive," and " Chugaeri," a forward modified somersault, have been devised to classify this essential technique. They imply ability

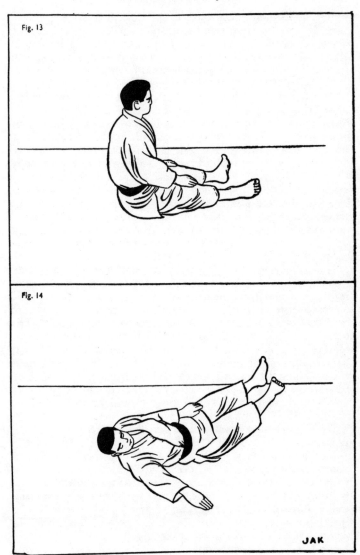

Fig. 13

Fig. 14

JAK

to fall forward and backward, to the right and left side and to execute the forward somersault fall. With the aid of the attached figures I shall now try to explain to you how most effectively you can practise these several methods until you feel sufficiently sure of yourself to try them out in Randori with your partner.

In the first place lie on your back on the mats at full length. Now bring your right hand and arm across your chest with the hand twisted so that the palm is held outwards. Raise your head slightly. Then beat the mat with your right hand and under forearm at a comfortable angle with your right side of between, say thirty and forty-five degrees. Twist your body slightly to the right as you do this. Duplicate the movement with your left hand and under forearm similarly twisting your body to the left side while so doing. Having mastered the movement repeat it rapidly alternately with right and left hand and arm, as described. It is astonishing what force can be put into the beat with the hand and arm on the mat once the most convenient angle has been secured.

Next sit upright on the mat with your legs stretched out. Now fall backwards and as you do so hit the mat first with your right hand and forearm held as before at about an angle of 30 to 45 degrees with your body. Then repeat this movement but using your left hand and forearm to beat the mat. The blow with your right hand should synchronize with a slight twist of your body to the right and the blow with your left hand with a slight twist of your body to the left. In all cases when falling backwards be careful to keep your head well forward so that it does not strike the mat. If you fix your eyes on the knot of your belt your head should be in the correct position (Figs. 13and and 14).

In the next stage practise falling backwards from a squatting posture slightly to right and left as before (Figs. 15 and 16).

Finally, practise the fall from a standing position. Lower yourself with your left leg and as you touch the mat beat it with your right hand and under forearm; then lower yourself with your right leg and beat the mat with your left hand and under forearm. The percussion of hand and mat acts as a spring to soften impact by absorbing most of the shock. In demonstrations of Kata or prearranged forms this practice never fails to impress the spectators who often marvel by what alchemy the seeming victim escapes broken bones (Figs. 17-21).

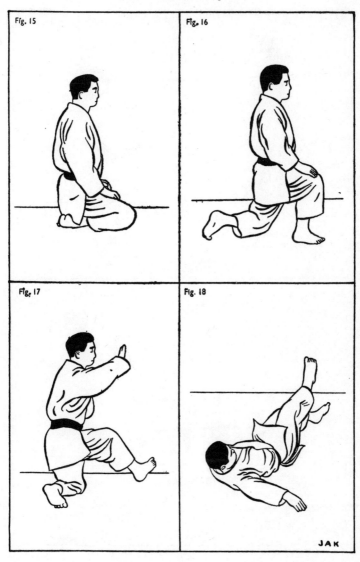

Fig. 15   Fig. 16   Fig. 17   Fig. 18

JAK

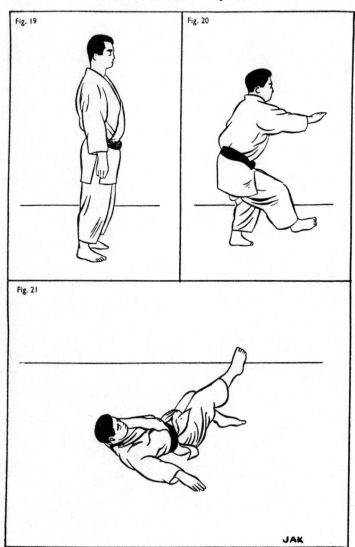

Fig. 19

Fig. 20

Fig. 21

JAK

In falling forward pay attention to the position of your hands as they hit the ground or mat. They should rest on the mat with the finger-tips turned in at about 45 degrees in order to ensure that your elbows are correctly bent so as to avoid injury. Begin by lying on your stomach with your hands in the above-mentioned position and the tips of your toes on the ground. Then repeatedly straighten and bend your elbows alternately until your joints are sufficiently strong to sustain the impact from a standing position (Figs. 22-24).

Next practise falling sideways. Support your body by placing your hand on the falling side on the mat with your finger-tips turned inwards so that your elbow bends in the right way (Fig. 24 (D)).

Study of the attached figures will better help you to get the hang of the necessary movement than many lines of letterpress description.

Lastly we come to the forward somersault or Chugaeri which calls perhaps for more rehearsal than the preceding movements.

Stand with your right foot a little forward. Then bend down and place your right hand between your legs with fingers pointing inwards and your left hand lightly resting on the mats in front of your left foot. Lower yourself still further in such wise that the back part of your head and right shoulder in obedience to the inward turn of your right hand and arm comes into contact with the mat. Synchronize this position with an energetic forward roll with legs and waist. Keep your body conveniently curved and your head well forward. Just as the movement reaches completion beat the mat with your free left hand and under forearm as strongly as possible. After a few attempts the momentum of your forward roll with the help of the hand beat will bring you to your feet (Figs. 24 (A), 24 (B) and 24 (C)).

It is advisable to practise the Chugaeri with the sequence reversed, i.e., with your left hand and arm lowered until your left hand is held between your legs and you do the forward roll from the back of your head and left shoulder. The beat in this case is made with your free right hand and forearm. As proficiency is acquired by frequent practice you should eventually reach a stage at which you can without fear convert the movement into a veritable forward somersault, hardly touching the mat with your hands or alternatively you can execute the

Fig. 22

Fig. 23

Fig. 24

JAK

movement with a flying start instead of from a stationary stance.

It is reassuring to realize that the breakfall can be more easily performed in Randori with an opponent than when attempted alone. Thus assume that your opponent throws you from the right natural posture, that is, with his right hand grasping your left lapel and his left hand holding your right sleeve about the back of the elbow, as your body falls towards your opponent's left and your own original right side when facing your opponent, you instinctively relinquish your left hand grip on your opponent's right sleeve and with your freed hand and forearm beat the mat in such wise that they act as a spring and break the force of your fall. Conversely, if you are thrown from the left natural posture, your right arm and hand are freed and beat the mat as your fall towards your opponent's right and your own original left side. If the breakfall has been correctly executed, the beat on the mat with your free hand and forearm will take place a split second before your torso becomes recumbent on the mat.

A golden rule to be observed in all such cases : *Always rise to your feet facing your opponent.* Failure to observe this rule may very well expose you to the danger of a chokelock applied from behind you before you have time to get up.

If space permits you cannot do better than do a few preliminary breakfalls before beginning your daily Judo practice. Apart from the value of the breakfall as a precautionary measure against broken bones, it is intrinsically a splendid warming-up exercise in anticipation of either Randori or contest.

Butsukari

Attainment of proficiency in any Judo technique depends upon a prodigious number of repetitions estimated by Kodokan experts to run to at least a hundred thousand each ! It will be clear from this postulate that non-professionals or persons unable to devote most of their waking hours to Randori, Kata and Shiai cannot hope to achieve perfection in all the throws of the Judo repertoire, comprising several hundreds. Their aim should therefore be to master even as few as two, three or four in preference to contenting themselves with merely superficial knowledge of many. And it is noteworthy that at the famous Kodokan the victorious methods exemplified in actual contest

Fig. 24 (A)

Fig. 24 (B)

Fig. 24 (C)

JAK

can be narrowed down to perhaps hardly more than half-a-dozen all told.

As a short-cut to mastery of a chosen throw the Kodokan has devised what is called Butsukari (from the verb "butsu" to hit or strike and the verb "karu" (to reap). This takes the form of an exercise between two pupils, one of whom applies the selected throw against his unresisting partner but only by means of Kuzushi up to the point of Tsukuri or the destruction of his partner's posture or balance without actually completing the throw or Kake. Whereas several hundred repetitions of a throw in Randori against your victim would be not only exhausting for you but decidedly painful for your victim, recourse to the economy of Butsukari overcomes this objection and enables you to familiarize yourself with the relevant technique until you have, so to say, gained the "feel" of it and its subsequent execution in Randori or contest becomes almost a reflex action.

Kumi-kata (Methods of Taking Hold)

Methods of taking hold of an opponent's jacket or belt, in Japanese terminology Kumi-kata, are of great importance for the successful application of a throw and should therefore be carefully studied by the serious judoka. I give them here in their most convenient order.

For obvious reasons the lapels of the jacket most frequently lend themselves to your grasp.

Normal or regular grip (Jun-ni toru tokoro) : The thumb is on the inside of your opponent's lapel and the four fingers are on the outside. As a general rule this form of hold would be applied with your right hand against your opponent's left lapel and your left hand against his right lapel, but can of course be applied with the same hand—right or left—against his right or left lapel respectively, although such form of a hold is less usual save in the case of the chokelocks to be later described.

Reverse grip (Gyaku ni toru tokoro) : The thumb is on the outside of your opponent's lapel and the four fingers are inside it. And in this instance actual experiment will convince you that your right hand will usually be holding your opponent's right lapel and your left hand his left lapel. As will appear later, this reverse grip comes into play when you are applying

Fig. 24 (D)

JAK

Fig. 25

Fig. 26

one of the most powerful and deadly chokelocks in the Judo repertoire.

In the case of the belt or sash three main holds are operative. Thus in the normal or regular grip your thumb is inside and your fingers are outside the belt which usually means that you are holding your opponent's *rear* belt with either your right or left arm encircling his waist.

Under or reverse side grip (Ura de toru tokoro): In the so-called under or reverse side grip your right or left hand is passed underneath your opponent's belt with your four fingers overlapping from beneath and your thumb resting conveniently approximately upon your first and second fingers.

Outer grip (Omote de toru tokoro): Your thumb passes underneath your opponent's belt and your four fingers over it with the back of your hand uppermost.

And in this context it is well once more to warn you against too tight a grip until the actual moment of throwing, for the reasons cited in my introductory remarks.

Defence and Counter Technique (Fusegi and Kaeshiwaza)

In this course of instruction I cannot undertake to provide detailed defences and counters for all the many methods described. Not even authoritative Japanese textbooks on Judo with which I am familiar do that. Where advice under this head seems likely to be useful and more readily understood, I have given it in its proper place. On the whole, however, I am satisfied that a wealth of detail, lacking much photographic demonstration, would tend only to confuse the student. The relevant defences and counter measures are more easily explained and to my mind of more practical value in Katamewaza or Groundwork and in such cases I have done my best to achieve comparative clarity.

On the other hand, in the sphere of Tachiwaza or throws effected from a standing position, the student can hardly do better than train himself to think quickly and if possible a split second ahead of his assailant so that he can anticipate the projected throw. Then his safest course for the purpose of nullifying it is to *shift his weight* and in this manner oppose what is called in Judo parlance a "floating" leg to his attacker's Tsukuri or would-be destruction of his balance. As I have already tried to explain, the right moment for Kake or actual throwing is when your opponent's weight is on the point of resting on his leading foot but before it has been completely shifted to that foot. It thus goes without saying that in Judo timing is of primary importance. It is not denied that a powerful judoka may succeed in throwing a weaker opponent by attacking his leg after the transfer of weight has been completed, but even so the successful throw cannot fairly be regarded as a faithful exemplification of the rationale of the art, and a Japanese Yudansha critic's curt comment upon such a demonstration would usually be "*Muri da!*" ("It's unreasonable!") Obdurate persistence in ignoring this basic principle and in placing more reliance upon "beef" than skill may do the offender irreparable harm in his pursuit of the coveted Black Belt and should be sternly renounced once and for all.

Of course all Judo instructors make every allowance for infringement of this basic principle when the student is engaged in contest. Until the judoka has become thoroughly seasoned by frequent participation in competition, being a prey to natural excitement and nervousness he is bound to lapse in this respect. On the other hand, the express purpose of so-called Keiko or practice in Randori is to afford the pupil an opportunity to cultivate true Judo under conditions that will enable him to practise his selected throws without being deeply concerned whether or not his opponent counters him. Randori (Free Exercise or Practice) and Shiai (Contest) are two different things and ought not to be confused. Of course there is nothing to prevent partners in Randori from agreeing on the spot to improvise a purely private contest as a friendly test of superiority, but unless the aspiring judoka is prepared and willing to risk being thrown when trying out some particular technique his progress in the art is likely to be retarded. Many of the most formidable Japanese Yudansha of my acquaintance when I attended the Kodokan in Tokyo thought nothing of being thrown in Randori, but when engaged in contest there was a very different story to tell!

Contact in Judo (Mitchaku suru)

The word "contact" does not merely imply "one against the other" but indicates also a state in which two bodies rest in intimate liaison during an action—pulling or pushing—without the rhythm being broken.

Thus in a case where, for example, you want to draw your opponent in order afterwards to push him, the contact between your body, your hand and the body of your opponent through the intermediary of the judogi must be included in your action without ever being broken by slackening of the fabric. Yet this continuous pressure does not mean continuous force or intensity.

The action of throwing in Judo is often likened to the ballistics of a sling, the body being the stone and the judogi the leather. The stone is hurled by centrifugal force of the gyratory movement without the leather being for an instant slackened before the final relinquishment.

In Judo, whatever may be the directions towards which the hand successively directs the body, in order to unbalance it and then throw it, the contact "body-hand-fabric" must also be without break if maximum efficacy is to be attained.

Before beginning Kuzushi or disturbance of balance it is vital to establish contact, if it has not already been established, and between the sequence Kuzushi-Tsukuri-Kake the most critical moment is that of the transition Tsukuri-Kake where the most common fault is for the judoka to relax contact for a brief instant, and that instant may be utilized by one's opponent to recover his balance or to counter attack.

You should establish this contact of the wrists but by a gentle continuous action " as for fishing," according to the expression of Mr. Tabata, 10th Dan of the Kodokan. Any rigidity or shock would upset the rhythm of the action and warn the other; that is why, in his description of the natural posture (Shizentai), Mr. Hashimoto, 9th Dan, advocates "without strength in the hands."

The ease and freedom of movement of a Master, his adaptation of opportunities and the consummation of his throw depend as much upon his posture (shisei) as upon his contact. Between rest and action the quality of his hold is not subject to any slackening and the throws are effected without jerky abrupt tuggings or shocks. His strength is drawn into his Tanden or abdomen, transferred fully from his body into his hands not by local employment of each hand or of the arm but of a single block; then from his hands on to the body of the other without interruption. When you have realized all the importance of contact, all sensation of slackening or of shock in your movement will be regarded as a rupture of contact and a disunion in your bodily action. The essential qualities of Judo reside in the execution of throws with finesse, without the expenditure of strength, joined to an irresistible rhythm. No less a person than Trevor Leggett, 5th Dan of the Kodokan, and the highest ranking non-Japanese Yudansha to date, has aptly epitomized the rationale of the art in his saying that Judo is *not* a test of strength and endurance but *par excellence* of skill.

INSTRUCTION II

SELECTED STANDING THROWS (TACHIWAZA) OF HAND TECHNIQUE (TEWAZA)

ADHERING to the sequence of classification given in my introductory remarks, I shall now try to describe what I regard as
the more useful throws of the Hand Technique (Tewaza) from
a standing position (Tachiwaza). The first throw on my list is :

Ukiotoshi (Floating Drop)

You engage your opponent in the customary right natural
posture (migi-shizentai), i.e., your right foot slightly advanced,
your right hand holding his left lapel in the normal grip, as
described in my first lesson, and your left hand his right sleeve
near the elbow. He engages you in the same posture. From
this stance you retreat seven or eight inches and disturb your
opponent's balance towards his right front corner. In the
demonstration of Nage-no-Kata or prearranged forms of
throwing, fifteen in number, the victim's (Ukete) balance is not
finally broken until the third attempt. Theoretically, of course,
the process of pulling your opponent forward towards his right
front corner could be prolonged almost indefinitely, but in
Randori or in actual contest you would naturally try to apply
Kake or the actual throw as soon as possible and would not, if
successful, allow your antagonist to recover his natural posture.
Instead you should suddenly drop on your left knee so that the
centrifugal force of this move draws your opponent forward far
more violently than he had expected and he can no longer
retain his natural posture but instead finds his balance broken
towards his right front corner. Lastly, from the direction of
your left side to your rear his falling body describes a curve
and he lands on the mat with his back. (Fig. 25).

Although superficially regarded this technique may impress
the student as fairly easy, it is not really so and in fact exempli-
fies much of the fundamental rationale of Judo, more particularly the efficacy inherent in the principle of not opposing
strength to strength but rather of seeming to give way only in

the end to lure the assailant to his own undoing. In a real fight, if rushed by a heavier and seemingly stronger adversary, you might resort to the Ukiotoshi to good purpose and throw him so heavily as to knock him out. Assiduous practice of the Ukiotoshi will confer upon you the knack of Kuzushi or disturbing balance from the natural posture when retreating before your opponent's advance. Analogously, try to master the same knack when pushing your opponent in the line of his pulling, always bearing in mind the principle of retreating slightly faster than you are pushed and advancing slightly faster than you are pulled. By carefully studying the most efficacious method of applying your strength to the greatest advantage and in the most vulnerable direction in both pulling and pushing, you will be most likely to foster and develop skill in Judo.

I am taking it for granted that having mastered this throw as executed from the right natural posture you will experience no great difficulty in applying it with the necessary adaptations from the left natural posture when needless to say you must drop on your *right* knee and your opponent is thrown towards your right side.

Seoinage (generally known as the " Shoulder Throw ")

Although this throw is one of the fifteen throws demonstrated in the Kodokan's Nage-no-Kata or Throwing Forms, I deem it more practical and useful to explain it as generally applied in Randori or Free Practice as being more in consonance with conditions of real life. Thus in the Nage-no-Kata the Seoinage is applied as a defence retort to an overarm blow delivered by your assailant, but unfortunately in a style which, I feel bound to say, no self-respecting thug with even the most elementary knowledge of boxing would dream of adopting!

As in the case of nearly all other throws I shall confine my description to the right natural posture or migi-shizentai in which you are holding your opponent's left lapel with your right hand and his right arm in the region of the elbow with your left hand, and with your right foot slightly advanced. Once you have grasped the application of a particular throw from the right natural posture you should try the same throw from the left natural posture or hidari-shizentai in which you hold your opponent's right lapel with your left hand and his left arm at the elbow with your right hand, and with your left foot slightly advanced. It is certainly most advisable that although almost inevitably you will develop a preference for one or other side, you should try to accustom yourself to attacks in both directions in automatic response to your opponent's varying movements which may invite your attempted Kuzushi, Tsukuri and Kake on either side. Restriction of a given technique to only one side, let us say while you are engaged in the right natural posture, may conceivably bring in its train the loss of valuable opportunities for applying a throw. Below are my descriptions of the more important variants of the Shoulder Throw which bears some family resemblance to the well-known Cumberland Flying Mare but is, I think, a far more "scientific" version.

A favourable opening for an attempt at this throw may present itself when you have succeeded in disturbing your opponent's posture or balance towards his right front and he is tilted somewhat forward with the weight of his body inclining on his tiptoes. See that your left hand is holding his right sleeve from the inside. Now raise his right arm somewhat and then pivoting on your right foot turn your body so that that foot is brought to the inner side of his right foot and pointing in the same direction. This movement should synchronize with the relinquishment of your hold on his left lapel with your right hand. Thrust that hand and arm under your opponent's right armpit to grip his right upper sleeve or right shoulder. Your back will be tilted somewhat backwards and kept in close contact with your opponent's chest and abdomen. Your knees should not be bent, only the upper part of your body ought to be inclined forward in the fashion of a wheel hub. Your opponent is then lifted on to your back and with the use of both your hands you bring him over your right shoulder and let him drop athwart your front. (Figs. 26 and 27). The reason why you are instructed to keep your left-hand hold on his right arm *inside* the crook of his elbow is in order to forestall a possible attempt to choke you with that arm in the very act of your lifting him from the mat in the hope of hurling him over your right shoulder. Of course when this particular throw is demonstrated in the formal Nage-no-Kata this danger does not arise but in Randori and still more in a real fight it might very well do so !

In a second variant of this throw you retain the grip with your right hand on your opponent's left lapel, then lower your body slightly, bend your right elbow and slip your forearm deeply under your opponent's right armpit. Your left-hand hold on his right arm is much the same as also the remainder of the throw.

It is sometimes easier to let go the hold on your opponent's left lapel with your right hand, transfer the hold with that hand to his *right* lapel in the reverse grip, as described in the first lesson, and from this position, with bent elbow, insert your right forearm underneath his right armpit and from this point proceed as in the first method.

In yet a fourth method, should you feel that your opponent's right-hand hold on your left lapel can be easily shaken off, break his posture towards his *left* front corner; then with your left hand sweep away his right hand; next advance your *left* foot to the inner side of his *left* foot and pointing in the same direction. Using that foot as axis turn your body to your right side and thrusting your left arm beneath his left armpit grasp his upper left sleeve or shoulder and throw him this time over your *left* shoulder. Your *right* hand grips his left sleeve near the curve of the elbow to thwart any attempt on his part to choke you from behind. It may be added that this left-hand variant of the Seoinage is not often seen in practice, but any judoka really proficient in it would surely prove a dangerous antagonist in contest.

The Seoinage or Shoulder Throw can be usefully applied by a short judoka against a taller opponent.

I need hardly say that for the successful accomplishment of every throw synchronization of the various movements is all important.

As regards methods of countering (Kaeshiwaza in Japanese), we have it on the authority of no less an expert than Takahashi Hamakichi, 8th Dan of the Kodokan, that this throw has no counter or is difficult to counter. However, although no doubt this contention may be true when the throw is applied by a highly skilled exponent, I would point out that it is sometimes possible to nullify the completion of this throw at the very moment of Kake, when the upper part of your body is already shouldered by your opponent, by passing your left leg round your opponent's left waist and hooking your left foot in his groin. If you succeed in this move a clean throw is no longer possible and as a rule you may expect to roll to the mat together with your opponent. True this is a somewhat crude, rough and

Fig. 27

Fig. 28

Fig. 29

Fig. 30

JAK

ready method but if it proves effective why should you worry?

My next selected throw of the Hand Techniques is called:

Taiotoshi (Body Drop)

Unlike the Seoinage or Shoulder Throw just described, the Taiotoshi is a throw equally suited to both the tall and short judoka. Other advantages are that openings for its application are comparatively frequent as, for example, when your opponent advances, retires or remains motionless, and that it is not easily countered. Confining myself to action in the right natural posture an opportunity occurs when your opponent moves his right foot forward, when he moves his left foot forward, when he leans forward from the fundamental natural posture (Shizenhontai), when he stretches his body or when you surprise him with any sudden movement.

Tsukuri or fitting action for attack, otherwise destruction of your opponent's balance, can be effected when your opponent advances his right foot and just before he plants it on the mat. Pull him in the direction of his foot. If your tsurikomi or lift-pull is successful he loses his balance and is hoisted on to the tips of his toes. Almost simultaneously place your right foot in front of his right foot and withdraw your left foot a little to the rear. In order not to jeopardize your own balance take care not to stretch your legs unduly. Your left hand holding your opponent's right sleeve is pulled towards your stomach as you turn your body to the left, while your right hand draws his body over your own. Your right arm from the shoulder to the elbow should be held tightly in contact with your body, and your centre of gravity is at this stage above your left foot. Be careful not to lift your head so as not to hollow your back, and do not turn your hip too much to the left. Your right leg crossing your opponent's right leg may be poised on the toes of that foot. The actual throw (Kake) is effected from this stance and at that moment your body from the right foot to the right shoulder should be as straight as a stick. It does not really matter whether your body is leaning against your opponent's or away from it. In the former instance the throw may almost give the impression of a hip or loin technique, but actually, of course, the dynamic impulse emanates from your hands. (Fig. 28).

Seoiotoshi (Shoulder Drop)

Openings for the application of this hand throw are comparatively rare, but since it can sometimes be resorted to against a short opponent ordinarily less vulnerable to the Seoinage or Shoulder Throw already described, I have deemed it advisable to include a brief explanation of it here.

An opportunity to attempt it may occur when such an opponent is standing upright in the right natural posture. With your left hand take firm hold of your opponent's belt with the under grip in the region of his right front corner and with your right hand grasp his right inner sleeve. Now while drawing his body with your left hand on his belt twist yourself to the left with your back turned to his front. Simultaneously bring your right elbow to the outer side of your opponent so that your right shoulder becomes inserted under his right armpit. Now drop on to your left knee and with the co-ordinated action of your left hand gripping your opponent's belt and your right arm and elbow engaging his right arm, draw him over your right shoulder and land him on the mat in front of you in much the same fashion as in the case of the Seoinage. (Fig. 29).

One legitimate criticism which can be adduced against this throw is that in a real struggle on, let us say, a street pavement, the drop to your knee might prove unduly painful or even result in injury to the knee-cap.

Kataguruma (Shoulder Wheel)

As in other cases I shall confine my explanation to the application of this throw from the right natural posture. Your aim while manœuvring is to break your opponent's balance towards his right front corner. The action of your hands and arms in bringing about this result in any direction is technically known as a "tsurikomi", literally "lift-pull", by which is meant that your hand holding your opponent's lapel effects the required lift while simultaneously your hand holding his sleeve effects the required pull. This action is designed to draw your opponent as close as possible to you. It may very well cause him to lean forward somewhat. At that moment you should slightly advance your right foot, simultaneously lower your hips, insert your right hand deeply between your opponent's thighs and with the same hand firmly grip his right thigh. Then with your left hand lightly raise his right upper arm and thrust your head and neck under his right armpit. With the combined strength of your right arm grasping his right thigh and your neck hoist him on to your shoulders. From this

position lower your head and neck and instantly drop him to
the mats in front of you or alternatively towards your left
side. (Fig. 30).

Obiotoshi (Belt Drop)

Although this hand technique can hardly be said to satisfy
the requirements of general elegance and is rarely demonstrated in friendly contest, it may commend itself to a judoka
with exceptionally strong arms and if brought off successfully
in a genuine rough and tumble would be calculated to deprive
your opponent of all interest in the subsequent proceedings.

As before I shall assume that you are engaging your
opponent in the right natural posture. An opening for the
application of this rough throw may occur if he shows a tendency to protrude the lower part of his body when you pull
him, perhaps because his waist and loins are insufficiently
lowered. At this juncture with your right hand seize with the
under grip the right front of his belt and with a slight lifting
motion draw him towards your abdominal region while simultaneously with your left hand you dash off his right hand
holding your left lapel and from your opponent's right armpit
turn the lower part of your body towards his rear so that his
buttocks are brought in contact with your stomach and the
right back corner of his ribs or side becomes flush with the left
front corner of your ribs. Place your left foot to the back of
your opponent's left heel and pass your left arm slantwise across
his front from his right breast to his left waist. In this posture
you should be holding your opponent under your left armpit.
Then with your stomach slightly press and lift his buttocks
until his body is somewhat tilted to the rear and supported by
your left hip or waist. Then with the combined force of the
upper half of your body and your arms drop your opponent
heavily to your rear. (Fig. 31).

In a real fight you need have no compunction about falling
alongside and jabbing him in the solar plexus with your left
elbow and so knock him out for the count.

Sotomakikomi (Outer Winding Throw)

I should warn you that this particular hand throw can be
very violent and ought therefore to be carefully practised
against your Judo partner if unpleasant shock or even bodily
injury is to be avoided.

Fig. 31

Fig. 32 (A)

Fig. 32 (B)

Fig. 33

JAK

It may happen that before you have actually come to grips with your opponent and while he still seems uncertain about what stance to assume he stretches out his right arm and tries to seize your left lapel or shoulder. Or while actually engaged in the right natural posture he may with his right hand take hold of your left lapel or shoulder and with his left hand hold your right sleeve while at the same time you may sense that his general stance is somewhat insecure. Moreover if in these circumstances you draw him with your body he may in Judo parlance " float " forward. Availing yourself of this opening for attack you should with your left hand take firm hold of your opponent's right lower sleeve and with a slight drawing motion attach it snugly to your body. Advance your right foot to within a foot of his right front corner. Simultaneously with your right hand and arm hug his right elbow from above. Now using your advanced right leg as an axis or fulcrum turn your body from right to left. Your left leg should be shifted in between your opponent's right leg and your own right leg and held slightly bent, your buttocks protruded so that close contact is effected between your left flank and the right front corner of the upper half of your opponent's body. In this position his right arm and body are, as it were, wound over your body so that if you turn your body and fall to your right the resultant impetus carries him over you in such wise that from his abdomen to his flank he is pinned to the mat by your back. You should hit the mat approximately with your right side. As in every other throw try to co-ordinate your movements and to observe the correct sequence. (Fig. 32 (A).)

From this brief description it will be evident that if you land too heavily and clumsily upon your prostrate opponent you may as likely as not break one or more of his ribs. I have in my day at the Kodokan known such a thing to happen.

An equally effective variant of the Sotomakikomi is known as the Uchimakikomi or Inner Winding Throw.

The opening for this variant is virtually identical with that of the Sotomakikomi as also is its entire rationale, so to speak. The difference begins at the point of Kake or complete destruction of your opponent's balance, i.e. the actual throw. Thus instead of taking hold of your opponent's right arm with your right arm from *over* the elbow you do so from under his arm, while with your left hand, back uppermost, you seize his right wrist. Then as in the case of the Sotomakikomi you gradually turn your body over which your opponent's body is wound. The relevant changes in the position of your feet are the same as also is your final fall to your right which lands your victim under you on the mat. (Fig. 32 (B).)

Both these throws could be effectively used in a real fight and intensely enough to knock out your adversary.

Formerly the Sotomakikomi and Uchimakikomi were classified under the heading of Yokosutemiwaza or Throws in a lying Position with one's Side on the Ground, but they have now been relegated to the Hand Techniques, as above.

INSTRUCTION III

SELECTED STANDING THROWS (TACHIWAZA) OF LOIN OR WAIST TECHNIQUES (KOSHIWAZA)

In this category are included some of the most spectacular throws of the copious Judo repertoire. The first on my list is :

Ukigoshi (Floating Loin or Waist)

By way of a change from my general plan of describing throws from the right natural posture, I shall explain the Ukigoshi as performed from the left natural posture, as is customary in the Nage-no-Kata or fifteen formal prearranged throws of the Kodokan.

In the Nage-no-Kata an opening for application of this method is provided when your partner styled Ukete or Receiver aims a blow at your head with his right fist. In Randori or free practice, however, you should attempt it from a left natural posture after successfully breaking your opponent's balance towards his front or generally if you contrive to make his body " float " forward in a somewhat unbalanced manner. At that moment advance your left foot a pace and as you turn your body to the right encircle your opponent's waist from his right side with your left arm and manœuvre so that your left foot is placed just on the inner side of his left foot and pointing in the same direction. Your rear waist and central part of your back should be brought into the closest possible contact with your opponent's chest and abdomen. With your right hand you grip your opponent's left upper sleeve from the outside. From this stance swiftly twist your loins from left to right and drawing him strongly forward throw him to the mat in front of you. The position of your right foot may safely be left to your discretion, but approximately it might be slightly outside your opponent's right foot. In some ways the Ukigoshi is reminiscent of the cross-buttock practised in the Cumberland style of wrestling but in essentials less crude and more thoroughly elaborated. (Fig. 33).

Your attention is particularly called to the following salient factors :

Inasmuch as this technique is to be applied when your opponent's body is " floating " forward and he is thrown chiefly with the power of the twist of your loins, your right hand holding his left sleeve is employed merely to help in drawing him forward. In the second place, while your left foot is advanced and when your body is turned, be careful not to lower the latter or to bend your waist and loins forward, but rather to incline them backwards, and it is highly important that your hips and back should be in close contact with your opponent's chest and stomach. If your body is lowered and your waist and loins are bent forward, the efficacy of the twist of your loins will be impaired. Thirdly, seeing that the object of your encirclement of your opponent's body, in this case with your left arm, is to maintain unbroken contact between your two bodies, you should avoid gripping either his belt or any other part of his clothing. If your two bodies are not linked together, even if the twist of your loins seems adequate, its effect will fall short of what is necessary to ensure a clean throw. Fourthly, when encircling your opponent with your left arm, the inner side of the arm from finger-tips to upper sleeve should hug your opponent's waist in the region of his rear belt, and at the time of touching him with your loins or when twisting the latter it is important that your two bodies should not be separated. Thus, although accompanying the twist of your loins a sensation of twisting and lifting may be imparted to your left arm, this is not for the sake of throwing your opponent but simply to prevent the loosening of your loins and waist.

Bearing these factors in mind you should experience no difficulty in converting this method to a right natural posture Ukigoshi when obviously your *right* arm must encircle your opponent's waist necessarily from his left side, your right foot must be brought to the inner side of his right foot and parallel therewith, and your left hand must seize his right upper sleeve from the outside. The twist of your loins must then be from right to left.

In contradistinction to the application of this technique in the formal throws, it is by no means easy to create an opportunity for its application in Randori or free practice. A manœuvre recommended by one of my greatest instructors, the late Sakujiro Yokoyama, is to push your opponent a little; then if he pushes against you in return promptly try to make him "float" forward by a combined drawing and lifting movement. It will then be optional on your part whether to attempt a left or right loin attack. If you contemplate a left loin attack, relinquish your right hand hold on your opponent's left lapel, and if you do not grip his left sleeve or elbow from the outside he may inadvertently touch your left thigh with his left hand and his body inclining forward he may try to recover himself by advancing his left leg when he will be exposed to encirclement with your left arm.

A forward "floating" movement on your opponent's part may sometimes be induced by applying the palm, say of your right hand very gently to the vicinity of his rear belt and surreptitiously lightly pressing and lifting him from the rear; then if you fall back a pace or two your opponent may unconsciously "float" forward when you should instantly try to effect a throw with your right waist and loin.

Haraigoshi (Sweeping Loin)

Assuming that you are engaging your opponent in the right natural posture, by the application of a tsurikomi (lift-pull) on his left lapel and right sleeve you may succeed in breaking his balance towards his right front corner. Contrive to effect close contact between your torso from approximately your right armpit to the flank of your loins and your opponent's torso from his chest to his abdomen while simultaneously you thread your right arm under his left armpit, your hand touching his back. Draw him towards you with the weight of your body resting entirely upon your left leg as fulcrum. Let your right leg "float" for a moment and then with the outer edge of your right thigh touch your opponent's right front thigh; next almost simultaneously using your left toes as axis of rotation with a twist of your waist from right to left sweep his right thigh in the direction of your right side while your left hand holding his right arm pulls him in the direction of your left waist.

You need not be over pedantic regarding the point of impact between your right and your opponent's right leg. Your attacking leg should be somewhat stiffened and can effectively strike his leg even slightly beneath the knee, as recommended by Kudo Ichizo, 8th Dan of the Kodokan, who also makes the throw with the interior face of his calf touching the outer face of his opponent's calf.

Although the twist of waist and loins in the Haraigoshi resembles that of the Ukigoshi, yet in the former throw your loin is not so deeply inserted and so the force of the twist is not so great as that of Ukigoshi. Again, at the beginning of the Haraigoshi you are rather bending backwards in your opponent's direction. The weight of your body is then resting upon your right leg. But as you pull your opponent nearer, you transfer the weight of your body to your left leg. The angle of contact between your two bodies may be almost 90 degrees. As in this position it becomes easy for you to adhere closely to him with the right front corner of your chest and abdomen, you make the throw with the feeling that your armpit and right back corner of your flank are attached to him.

Kudo Ichizo referred to above describes his pet method of executing the Haraigoshi *to the left*, although he himself may be standing in the right natural posture! The more salient points of his explanation are the following : When my opponent pushes with his right hand he loses his balance to the front and to the left, and I place my right foot close to his right foot. In this case my right toes become the axis of rotation and I turn deeply to my right. With a movement of my left chest I push his right arm out of the way. At this stage his body is already touching my left buttock and I use my left leg stretched to throw him up in the air. This is the position of my left leg : slightly stiffened under my opponent's left knee, the interior face of my calf touching the outer face of his calf, the toes pointing downwards. In fact, when I turn on my right foot as an axis my opponent is already off the mat and floating in the air. I break his balance mostly with the movement of my right hand bringing him in the direction of his left front corner; the movement is the one you would do in swinging a stone at the end of a long string. All the following movements are to be made at the same time, the toes of your right foot serving as an axis, as you turn your body and place him on the back of your hip.

Tsurikomigoshi (Lift-pull) Loin. This throw can on occasion be successfully applied when your opponent has declined to be lured into a stance appropriate for either Haraigoshi or Ukigoshi, when, for example, he tends to bend backwards and

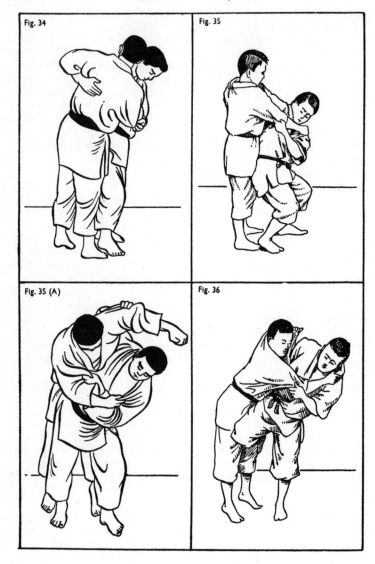

Fig. 34

Fig. 35

Fig. 35 (A)

Fig. 36

to protrude his stomach. Assuming that you are engaged in the right natural posture, apply a tsurikomi or lift-pull with both hands and then without relaxing your hold, while turning your body to your left and keeping both feet opposite and in line with those of your opponent, sink your rear waist to the level of your opponent's knees or even lower and in contact with them. From this stance, while strongly springing your waist, pull forward and downwards with both hands and capsize your opponent to your front (Fig. 35).

There is an effective variant of this throw known as the Sode-Tsurikomigoshi or Sleeve-Lift-Pull-Loin. As the name implies, with your right hand you grasp your opponent's left sleeve from outside at the elbow, and keep it well raised as you lower your waist and loins while with your left hand grasping your opponent's right sleeve you pull that arm downwards and simultaneously you fling up your loins and waist and throw him towards your right front. (Fig. 35 (A).)

Be careful to distinguish between the right and left natural postures when studying these techniques, since any mental confusion under this head is bound to nullify your execution of the given throw.

Hanegoshi (usually rendered "Spring-Hip Throw", although more correctly it means "Spring Waist or Loin")

This is undoubtedly one of the most spectacular and effective throws in the copious Judo repertoire, and at the same time one of the most difficult to master. Nor is it necessarily suited to the individual physical attributes of every Judoka. It is a throw in which your opponent is lifted through the impact of your bent leg while his body is leaning straight forward and not bent at the waist or knees.

Openings for its application arise (1) when your opponent's balance is broken forward in the fundamental natural posture; (2) when his balance is broken forward from a right natural posture; (3) when he moves back from a right natural posture and (4) when he moves to his right. For the moment I shall confine myself to the orthodox version of the throw as given by the late Sakujiro Yokoyama.

An opportunity for breaking your opponent's balance may occur if you have pulled him towards his right front corner, and he is tilted somewhat forward with the weight of his body imposed mostly upon his right leg. In an effort to recover himself he may advance his left foot when with your right hand you should lift-pull him upwards; then only slightly lowering your body bend your right knee and with its outer edge apply it above both your opponent's knees; with both your hands you impart a slight lift-pull motion to your opponent and, as it were, "spring lift" him to your right side.

It is important that the impetus of your throw should not be confined to your right leg; the operation of your loins is essential. Again, your left hand holding your opponent's right sleeve pulls downwards and your right hand grasping his left lapel presses and lowers in a direction opposite to that of the "spring lift" of your right leg. Thus with the harmonious co-ordination of your hands, loins and legs you can achieve the best results.

Ogoshi (Major Loin)

There is undoubtedly a close family resemblance between the Ukigoshi throw already described and the Ogoshi explained below. The most important difference between the two techniques is that whereas when you apply the Ukigoshi both you and your opponent are engaged in the right or left natural posture, when you apply the Ogoshi you do so from the *self-defensive posture either right or left*. Here I confine my description to the right self-defensive posture in which, you may remember, your knees are slightly bent and your waist is correspondingly lowered. Your opponent may also be standing in the right self-defensive posture or even in one somewhat approximating to the right natural posture. Now with your right arm lightly encircle his body from under his left armpit, the arm deeply inserted along his belt, the palm of your right hand touching his back as far behind as possible. Now with the palm of your right hand and with your arm apply a pressing lifting movement so that your opponent becomes tilted forward on his toes. At that moment swiftly lower your right loin a little, bring your right foot inside your opponent's right foot and parallel therewith and pointing in the same direction. Turn your body to the left so that the closest contact is effected between your loin and back and your opponent's stomach and chest. Now raise and twist your loin and with your left hand holding your opponent's right sleeve outside the elbow draw it towards your right breast. The impact of your back waist and loin against your opponent's body is low enough to lift him off

the mat. If these several movements have been properly synchronized your opponent should be thrown towards your right
front. (Fig. 37).

Ushirogoshi (Rear Loin)

The most suitable opening for an attempt at this throw is
when your opponent has tried unsuccessfully to score against
you with a loin or hip throw and without having disturbed
your balance has his back touching your abdominal region.
Say he has tried to bring off a throw with his right loin, lower
your body slightly while keeping it in close contact with your
opponent's, and from behind encircle his waist, your right hand
holding his right lower abdomen. Straighten your knees, raise
your waist a little and bend backwards while swinging your
opponent off the mat. His body should be lifted and tilted
backwards. Simultaneously, as you withdraw your body, you
let your opponent drop to the ground. If your opponent is
holding himself loosely and his legs are entangled with yours,
his body bent forward, it will be difficult for you to bring off
this throw. Instead his body should preferably be stiff and his
chest stuck out, thus facilitating application of this technique.
(Fig. 38).

Personally I do not rate the Ushirogoshi as a particularly
useful throw in a genuine "rough house", but since it figures
among the Koshiwaza or Loin Techniques I have thought it
advisable to include it here.

Koshiguruma (Loin Wheel)

This is, to my mind, a much superior throw to the foregoing.
Incidentally its *modus operandi* may commend it to pupils that
have some knowledge of Catch-as-Catch-Can methods.

Say that when engaged in the right natural posture you pull
on your opponent's right sleeve in an ostensible attempt to
break his balance towards his right front corner and in resisting
your move he turns towards his own left front corner, otherwise
in the direction of your right back. Nevertheless, failing to
revert to a natural posture he may tend to approach your right
waist. Availing yourself of the opportunity encircle his neck
with your right arm; then with your left hand pull his right
sleeve downwards along your chest and abdomen, slightly sink
your waist, pivot on your right foot to your left so that the
upper half of your body projects from your opponent's right

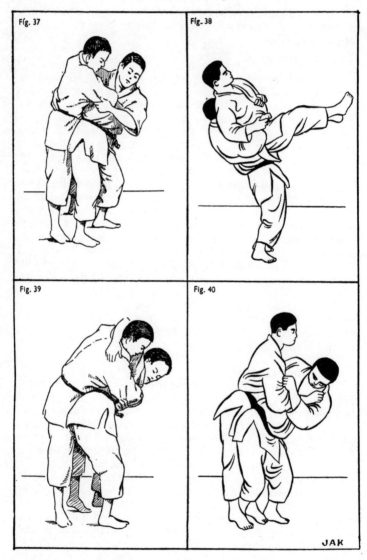

Fig. 37   Fig. 38

Fig. 39   Fig. 40

JAK

waist your left front waist almost flush with his right front waist. Then as you fling up your waist, simultaneously twisting the upper part of your body, your right arm wound round your opponent's neck is drawn forward with a circular movement; then with your left hand holding his right sleeve you pull downwards in such wise that his body is brought over your back and right side, and with your waist serving as an axle revolves as it were like a wheel and falls to the mat in front of you—hence the name " Loin Wheel ". This throw can easily be intensified so as, in case of self-defence, to throw one's assailant violently enough to knock him out. (Fig. 39).

Tsurigoshi (Lifting Hip Throw)

This is a technique in which, by way of a change, you help to break your opponent's balance with one hand holding his rear belt in the so-called regular or normal grip, that is, with your thumb inside and your four fingers overlapping the belt. There are actually two variants of this throw known respectively as the Otsurigoshi or Major Lifting Hip Throw and the Kotsurigoshi or Minor Lifting Hip Throw. The sole difference between these two forms is that in the Otsurigoshi you pass your right arm (if you are engaged in the right natural posture) *over* your opponent's left arm in order to grip his rear belt, whereas in the Kotsurigoshi you pass your right arm *under* his left arm. The appended description applies to the latter variant.

Engaged in the right natural posture your left hand holding your opponent's inside right sleeve should be extended while your right hand is passed under his left armpit to grasp his rear belt in the aforesaid normal hold. Should his body become slightly tilted forward, lift it with that hand and bring your right foot inside his right foot and pointing in the same direction. Turn your body from right to left and withdraw your left foot as far as possible to the rear outside your opponent's left leg. Your loins and back should be in the closest possible contact with your opponent's abdomen and chest. Pull down strongly with your left hand holding his right sleeve and couple this movement with the flinging up of your loins in co-ordination with the lift given by your right hand on your opponent's rear belt. If these movements have been properly synchronized your opponent ought to be hurled to the mat in front of you. It is sometimes possible to assist the momentum of the final Kaké or attack by flicking up your opponent's right leg with the lower

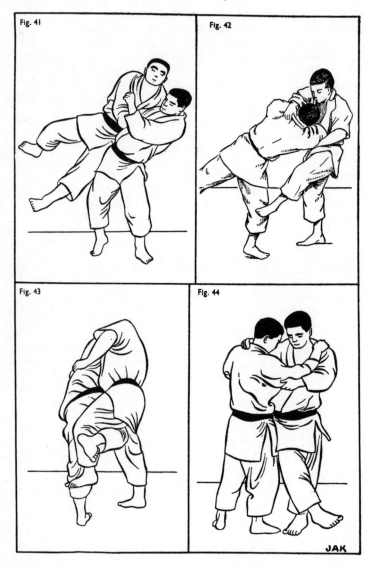

Fig. 41

Fig. 42

Fig. 43

Fig. 44

JAK

part of your right leg planted on its inner side. All in all by no means a bad throw. (Fig. 40).

Utsurigoshi (Transition Loin)

Assuming that you are engaged in the customary right natural posture and that planning to apply a contemplated technique your opponent has veered his left rear corner towards your right front corner or perhaps you have been able for some other reason to steal into his left rear corner, in such case promptly grip his torso with your right hand in the region of his waist, then slightly leaning backwards and with the help of your left hand holding your opponent's right sleeve lift him from the mat. In an effort to avoid being thrown he may shift both legs, when with the power of both your arms and waist you should swing him somewhat to the rear so that his body being turned towards your right rear affords a convenient opening for the application of a waist or loin technique. In that event, as in the case of the Ogoshi (Major Loin) twist your waist to the left, pull downwards strongly with your left hand gripping your opponent's sleeve, and throw him across your front. (Fig. 41).

I should not say that the Utsurigoshi figures among the more popular or frequently utilized throws, but when brought off it is decidedly pretty to watch.

The foregoing completes my selection of Koshiwaza or Loin Techniques. It is not, of course, absolutely exhaustive, but on the whole I think it comprises the throws of the greatest practical value to the average student.

INSTRUCTION IV

SELECTED STANDING THROWS (TACHIWAZA) OF FOOT AND LEG TECHNIQUES (ASHIWAZA)

I now come to the third and last in sequence but by no means least important branch in the classification of standing throws. Indeed this branch enjoys the distinction of including the two most popular and effective throws known to Judo, viz., the Uchimata (Inner Thigh) and the Osotogari (Major Exterior Reaping) which I shall presently describe. For instance, an analysis of the most famous Kodokan contests during the last twenty-five years reveals that the most victories were won by those two throws in the given order, i.e., Uchimata 897 or 16 per cent. and Osotogari 720 or 13 per cent. of all matches held. However, they were closely followed by the Haraigoshi with 560 wins or 10 per cent. and the Hanegoshi with 510 wins or 9 per cent.

To the same category belongs a series of what may be called ankle trips which admirably exemplify the basic principle of Judo and enjoy the additional advantage of imposing the minimum physical strain upon the performer. For that reason they are naturally favoured by older judoka who are beginning to feel unequal to the throws necessitating body torsion for the insertion of hips, loins or legs. For convenience of reference I shall describe the more important ankle trips last in this lesson. Study first then

Hizaguruma (Knee Wheel)

You are engaged in the right natural posture. While retreating make as if to break your opponent's balance towards his right front corner with the weight of your entire body carried on the ball of your right foot. This manoeuvre of course implies the orthodox tsurikomi or lift-pull with your right hand holding his left lapel and your left hand holding his right sleeve outside the elbow. Now maintaining a convenient distance from your opponent, your weight still resting on your right leg, apply the sole of your left foot gently to the outer edge of his

80

right knee-cap. Bend forward somewhat and twist your body to your left while simultaneously with your left hand holding his right sleeve you pull him towards you in the arc of a circle, reinforcing this movement with your right hand which grasps his left lapel. Given correct synchronization your opponent's body should turn on his knee as axle to his right front corner until his back hits the mat towards your left rear corner. (Fig. 42).

It is also possible while engaged in the right natural posture to throw your opponent by applying your *right* foot to his *left knee-cap*. If when you are trying to break his balance towards his right front corner he resists your attempt and pulls against you, let go your hold on his left lapel with your right hand and lightly grasp the inner side of his left sleeve in the region of the elbow and draw him in the direction of his *left* front corner. If he then advances his left leg and you judge that your Kuzushi has succeeded in its purpose, support the weight of your body this time upon your *left* foot and apply, as stated, the sole of your *right* foot to the outside of his *left knee-cap*. In this case, however, since the tension of your left hand grasping his right sleeve is somewhat lessened, your opponent is thrown chiefly with the combined help of your right hand, the curvature of your body and, of course, the percussion of your right sole against his left knee-cap. On no account should the contact between the sole of your foot and your opponent's knee-cap resemble a kick from which injury might arise.

Uchimata (Inner Thigh)

This is a magnificent throw which can be most effectively applied by a comparatively tall man against a shorter opponent.

As with all other standing throws the Uchimata can be executed to either right and left, and in view of its exceptional value as a fighting method I shall try to describe it in both these ways.

An indispensable preliminary to Kaké or final attack (the actual throw) is to break your opponent's balance to his front and compel him to bend forward with his legs spread more widely apart than usual. To this end it is a good plan to take a deep hold on his right lapel with your left hand. Make the fullest use of your weight in applying this Kuzushi. Now with your left foot as axis and left knee bent, concentrate, as it were, the whole strength of your body in your left toes looking in the direction in which your opponent's balance is broken, and simultaneously thrust your right thigh between his legs in such wise that its outside back is applied to the inside of his left thigh. Tense your body until it is almost parallel with the mat, stretch the inserted right leg and throw your opponent up into the air so that he falls towards your left rear corner. Before the impact of your attacking thigh takes place it is essential that close contact should be effected between the right side of the upper half of your body and your opponent's chest. When lifting your opponent into the air with the thrust of your right thigh be careful that your thigh touches the inner side or crotch of his thigh, otherwise not only will the efficacy of the throw be impaired but you will run the risk of injuring his testicles. (Fig. 43).

When the Uchimata is executed to the left you grip your opponent's left lapel very deeply with your right hand and so break his balance to his front until he is bent forward. This forward movement causes him to spread his legs and so facilitates the attack with your left leg. The outside of your left thigh is inserted and touches the inside of his right thigh. In this position stretch your left leg and throw for all you are worth.

Although the Uchimata is formally classified as a leg throw, yet when the leg slips well in between your opponent's legs it almost suggests a hip throw.

Osotogari (Major Exterior Reaping)

Another superb contest throw as demonstrated by the Kodokan statistics quoted above, and incidentally my own so-called Tokuiwaza or pet throw which I was accustomed to execute to the left of my opponent. Here again, considering its outstanding value, I shall try to explain both methods of attack.

A projected throw from the right natural posture presupposes the breaking of your opponent's balance to his right back corner as an indispensable preliminary manoeuvre. To this end you have to get as close as possible to his right side. There are two methods of achieving this aim, viz., by pulling your opponent to you by means of the appropriate tsurikomi (lift-pull) or by moving forward from your original stance. But after having effected the necessary approach by either method, one executes the throw itself (Kaké) in virtually the same manner. Use both hands in unison. With your right hand holding your opponent's left lapel high up at the shoulder push him backwards while with your left hand holding his right sleeve outside the elbow you pull him towards you and by means of the combined action of your hands bring his weight to bear upon his right heel. Advance your left foot to a point almost opposite or a little outside his right foot and support your entire body upon the toes of that foot. Raise your right leg and sweep the outer edge of your opponent's right thigh as forcibly as possible with the outer side of your right thigh. Synchronize this action with a downward pull of both hands on your opponent's right sleeve and left lapel respectively. If you are successful, your opponent should be hurled heavily to the mat. (Fig. 44).

Although in the orthodox version of this throw the sweeping movement with the right leg is made more or less sideways, no less an authority than Maeda Takesato, 8th Dan of the Kodokan, prefers to sweep to his own rear. However, this is a minor detail and in my opinion the best Judo policy is for the pupil to develop his own individual style and to beware of slavish standardization. Thus although in many demonstrated versions the attacker is shown bending slightly forward in the act of sweeping his opponent's thigh with his own, I was taught by the great Mifune, 10th Dan, to turn my head out-wards, to my left if executing the throw from the right natural posture, and to my right if executing it from the left natural posture, at the very moment of sweeping my opponent's thigh. My gaze would be directed upwards, approximately towards the ceiling. I always found that this movement seemed to impart more power to the sweep of the thigh.

When the Osotogari is executed from the left natural posture you must break your opponent's balance towards his *left* back corner. The weight of your body rests upon the toes of your right foot which is advanced to your own right opposite or a little beyond your opponent's left foot. You sweep your opponent's left thigh with your left thigh. In both cases the outer side of the thigh is the vehicle of impact. Since the sweep with the attacking thigh is made, properly speaking, against an opponent whose balance has been broken towards his right or left back corner, it might at first sight seem more logical that the back corner or angle of his thigh should be swept by the back corner or angle of the attacker's thigh—right or left, as the case may be. But if the attacker adopts this type of Kaké it will not prove sufficiently effective, and it is therefore advisable that the outer side of the attacker's thigh should be used to sweep the outer side of the opponent's thigh. It is in this respect that the Osotogari has to be differentiated from the Osoto-otoshi (Major Outer Drop) to be described later, seeing that in the execution of the latter throw the back of the thigh is driven down against the back of the opponent's thigh.

The Osotogari has been justly described by Maeda Takesato as " a grand and decisive throw " and by another expert as " a virile technique that has many followers ".

Ouchigari (Major Internal Reaping)

A description of this technique naturally follows the Osoto-gari above. Its popularity as a formidable and an effective contest throw is shown by its position in the Kodokan classification already quoted. It stands eighth on the list with 230 wins or 4 per cent. It was not so frequently practised in my day at the Kodokan and although mentioned among Ashiwaza or Leg and Foot Techniques in the late Sakujiro Yokoyama's well-known textbook on Judo, a copy of which he bequeathed to me before his lamented death very many years ago, it is not actually explained therein.

In these circumstances I offer no apology for basing my description in part upon data supplied by Oda Tsunetani, 9th Dan of the Kodokan, quoted in the valuable French publication " International Judo " (" Kokusai Judo") of which I have elsewhere availed myself.

A stance on the part of your opponent that invites attack by the Ouchigari is one in which his legs are rather more widely apart than usual. In the right natural posture your opponent will be holding your left lapel with his right hand. Retort by gripping the outside middle of his right sleeve with your left hand. If his legs are conveniently open, pull on his right sleeve, jump first on your left foot and then move forward your right foot, simultaneously contriving to strike his chest and face with your chest, now throw your right arm round his neck, thrust your right foot inside his left leg and from about the base of his thigh sweep it powerfully to your rear. Needless to say these movements must be carefully co-ordinated and synchronized. Your opponent may try to keep his balance or to counter by moving his hip backwards, but since your body strikes his chest and face he will not find escape so easy. Not a bad variant is to lift your opponent's right thigh with your left hand and at the same time sweep his left leg from within with your right leg, as already described. Your opponent's stance is further weakened if you can slant him on to his heels before the final attack. (Fig. 45).

Ashiguruma (Leg Wheel)

Although Kodokan contest statistics for the last twenty-five years give the Ashiguruma only 10 contest wins and place it twenty-sixth on the list of throws employed, I regard it as a decidedly elegant and effective technique and as such well worthy of study.

Say you are engaged in the right natural posture and that having pulled your opponent along a curved orbit towards your right side you try to break his balance towards his left front corner; as a result his body may be somewhat tilted forward with his left leg drawn back, and his natural posture in which his weight had been resting on his right leg may be disturbed. In an effort to recover it he may advance his left leg, in which case, taking advantage of the opportunity, the weight of your body supported on your left leg, you should bring your right flank into close touch with your opponent's left front corner, straighten your right leg and apply its edge obliquely from the region of his projected left front thigh to the knee of his right leg upon which his weight is resting, thereby blocking its advance. Your left hand holding his right sleeve should pull inwards and downwards while your right hand grasping his left lapel should press downwards with a slight turning movement. Simultaneously you must as it were sweep against your opponent's legs with your extended right leg which serves as an axle over which wheel-like his body rotates and falls to the mat. In executing this throw the foot of your outstretched right leg does not touch the ground on your opponent's right side, but is held some inches above it. (Fig. 46).

By way of a variant, you can sometimes, while still engaged in the right natural posture, use your *left* leg to effect this throw. To do this, let go your right hand hold on your opponent's left side lapel and swiftly substitute therefor a normal grip on his left upper sleeve from outside. Remember that the normal or regular grip is one in which your thumb—in this case your right—is on the inside and your four fingers are on the outside. Now if you pull your opponent with that hand towards his left front corner, he may very well advance his left leg with

Fig. 45

Fig. 46

JAK

Fig. 47

Fig. 48

his body slightly tilted and the weight resting on that leg. Taking advantage of this opportunity you simply reverse the order in which you used your right leg to apply the throw; instead this time you support your weight on your *right* foot and bring your *left* flank in close contact with your opponent's right front corner, straighten your left leg and stretch its outer edge slantwise from and against his right front thigh to the region of the knee of his left leg. Pull downwards and inwards with your right hand holding his left sleeve and press downwards with your left hand holding his right sleeve. If both your Tsukuri and Kaké have been successful, your opponent's body will rotate over your left leg as axle and land on the mat on your right.

Osoto-otoshi (Major Outer Drop)

Examination of Kodokan statistics reveals that as a popular contest throw the Osoto-otoshi ranks considerably higher than the Ashiguruma just described. Thus from a classification extending over twenty-five years it appears that the Osoto-otoshi scored as many as 158 wins as against only ten for the Ashiguruma. Certainly the Osoto-otoshi can easily be utilized as a decidedly violent throw to knock out an opponent in a real fight.

A favourable opportunity for application of the Osoto-otoshi may occur when you have succeeded in breaking his balance more towards his direct rear than his right back corner and when his weight is therefore resting more upon his right heel. Now with your own weight supported by your left leg, which you should bring opposite your opponent's right foot, assume a somewhat bent attitude, lift your right foot with bent knee and pass the foot and leg behind his right side; then promptly straighten the knee and with all your strength drive your right back thigh downwards against your opponent's right back thigh while simultaneously with both your hands you reinforce this momentum and throw him heavily backwards on the mat. In this movement you should push him backwards with your right hand holding his left lapel and pull him towards you with your left hand holding his right sleeve. (Fig. 47).

Although at first sight and superficially regarded there may seem to be some resemblance between the Osoto-otoshi and the Osotogari, closer scrutiny shows that they are actually two distinctive throws. Thus in the Osoto-otoshi the direction of your Kuzushi or disturbing balance is towards your opponent's direct rear with his weight resting upon his right heel, whereas in the Osotogari the direction of the disturbance of balance is towards his right back corner and his weight is resting on the back corner of his right foot. Again, in the Osoto-otoshi the direction of your advanced right leg is your direct front, whereas in the Osotogari it is your left side. In the Osoto-otoshi the actual throw is effected with your right back thigh against your opponent's right back thigh, whereas in the Osotogari it is effected more with the right back corner or side of your right thigh against the right side or back corner of your opponent's right thigh.

Osotoguruma (Major Outer Wheel)

Opportunities for bringing off this throw are comparatively infrequent, but if they do occur the resultant fall may sometimes be very heavy. On one occasion during contests at the Kodokan a particular friend of mine was taken unawares and thrown so drastically that he lost consciousness from concussion, but soon recovered and suffered no untoward consequences thereafter.

If, for example, while engaged in the right natural posture you have disturbed your opponent's balance towards his direct rear and the weight of his body is imposed upon the heels of both feet, you should bring up your left foot to a point more or less alongside the right side of your opponent's foot with the weight of your body resting on that leg. Then straightening your right leg pass it behind your opponent's right leg in such a manner that the back of it stretches from his right back thigh to his left back shin and in close contact therewith. Supplementing the impact of your right leg with the strength of both your hands, which execute the usual tsurikomi or lift-pull movement against your opponent, you bring him wheel-like over your right leg, which serves as an axle, until he falls to the ground.

Yama-arashi (Mountain Storm)

Although I can find no mention of this throw in the Kodokan classification of tricks used in contest during the last twenty-five years, it nevertheless enjoys a fair reputation and has been commemorated in a Japanese novel entitled " Sugata

Sanshiro", the name of the hero, a Judo champion who has made a speciality of this particular throw with which he defeats all and sundry.

To effect the Yama-arashi from the right natural posture you hold your opponent's right inner sleeve with your left hand but, in contradistinction to the customary right hand grasp of your opponent's left lapel you use that hand to grip his *right* lapel in the normal hold previously described. With this combination hold you draw him more and more towards his right front corner, and if in response he begins to incline towards that corner with the weight of his body resting on his right leg until he appears to be standing on tiptoe, you must bring your right back corner into close contact with your opponent's right front corner applying the edge of the shin of your right leg to the side of your opponent's right shin. Now with the full power of your right leg sweep his right leg and at the same time with your right hand make a lift-pull (tsurikomi) on his right lapel, while with your left hand holding his right sleeve you draw him with a circular movement and hurl him to the mat.

The foregoing completes my selection of throws executed with the leg. I shall now try to explain the more typical throws effected by the impact of either the ball of the foot or the inner arch of the foot against one's opponent's ankle or immediately above it. To the former category the suffix "harai" or "barai", derived from the Japanese verb "harau", meaning to sweep has been given, and to the latter the suffix "gari", derived from the Japanese verb "karu" meaning to mow or reap. All these ankle trips admirably exemplify the validity of the teaching that the moment to attack your opponent's foot is a split second before it is firmly planted on the mat but never either when it is so planted or when it is raised from the mat with the leg in which in Judo parlance is called a "floating" or buoyant state. First then

Ashihari (*Foot Dash or Sweep*)

Assume that you are engaged in the right natural posture. Your opponent may essay to disturb your balance towards your right front corner. Observing the basic principle of not opposing mere strength to strength you appear to yield to the pull he is applying and so contrive to advance more than he is retreating. Simultaneously with your arms holding your

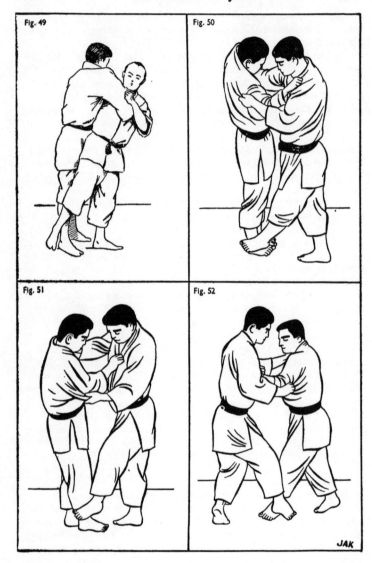

Fig. 49

Fig. 50

Fig. 51

Fig. 52

opponent's left lapel and right sleeve you make a lifting circular movement designed to raise him upward in order to break his balance towards his left back corner. But once his weight has been transferred from his right to his left foot it is too late to attack either of them because the right leg will be "floating" or buoyant and the left foot already on the mat. Indeed an attempt to sweep the right "floating" foot might quite easily expose you to the danger of a counter technique. Similarly if your opponent has transferred his stance from his left to his right foot, his weight wholly imposed upon the latter, an attempt to sweep that foot would be tactically bad and even though through sheer "beef" you did succeed in throwing your opponent, your method would run counter to the basic principles of Judo and should not be encouraged. On the other hand, if your opponent first withdraws his right foot, then in order to withdraw his left foot tries to transfer the weight of his body to his right leg but has not yet completed the transfer and his right foot is not yet quite planted on the mat, while his left leg is "floating", the moment is opportune for you to sweep his right ankle with the sole of your left foot. And as already said, you should reinforce these moves with the circular uplift exerted by your arms holding your opponent's lapel and sleeve. In that case, even should your opponent try to transfer his weight from his left to his right foot, the latter can be easily swept, as his body is inclined towards his right front corner. Be careful that the sweeping movement of your foot against your opponent's ankle does not degenerate into a kick from which pain and even injury might result. The sweep should be a firm steady pressure whose dynamic impulse is not confined to your leg and foot alone but includes the motive power emanating from the rest of your body and more especially from your saika tanden or lower abdominal region. This principle applies to virtually all Judo methods and cannot be too strongly impressed upon the earnest student of the art. (Fig. 50).

Okuri-Ashi-Harai (Pursuit-Foot-Dash or Sweeping Ankle Throw)

This too is quite a spectacular form of ankle attack. You should watch for an opportunity when your opponent's feet are in line and inclined to come together. If you are in the right natural posture and your opponent is moving up his right foot towards his left and, of course, before it is firmly planted, sweep that foot strongly with the sole of your left foot. At the same time lift him with both hands, wrists uppermost and arms held lengthwise. Lean slightly forward with your entire body raised on the toes. (Fig. 51).

Deashi-Harai (Advanced Foot Dash or Sweep)

As the name implies, the sweep with the sole of your foot is directed against your opponent's advanced foot—the right, if you are engaged in the right natural posture. An opening for recourse to this technique can occur when your opponent has advanced and moved his right foot rather more than usual to his left and there is a tendency for both his feet to come together. In that case when he is on the point of shifting his weight on to his right leg but has not yet entirely done so, you may advantageously attempt this trip. As in the previous throws described under this head, apply the sole of your left foot to the outside of your opponent's right ankle or about the back of his heel and simultaneously pull him with both your hands towards his right front corner until he falls. Be careful when executing this trip that through inadvertence your left inside ankle bone does not hit the right outer ankle bone or shin of your opponent with painful consequences to both of you. See that when making the sweep your left foot is sufficiently curved.

If you prefer to use your right foot in this method of attack, you can engage your opponent in the left natural posture, that is, with your left hand holding his right lapel and your right hand his left sleeve at the elbow. Then watch for the moment when he advances his *left* foot and tends to bring it up to his right foot. Then before the transfer of his weight to his left foot has been completed, sweep his left ankle with the sole of your right foot. (Fig. 52 illustrates the latter method).

Tsurikomi-Ashi (Drawing Ankle Throw)

Assume you are engaged in the right natural posture. Preserving the natural posture, much as in the case of the Uki-otoshi elsewhere described, while disturbing your opponent's balance towards his right front corner you withdraw a pace or two so that your opponent is pulled towards you and his body begins to incline forward while he endeavours to prevent his natural posture from being broken. If at this juncture you were suddenly to fall on your left knee and unexpectedly pulling your opponent you threw him, the technique would be the Uki-otoshi. However, in the case of the Tsurikomi-Ashi you should pull the upper part of your opponent's body somewhat more than the advance of his right leg so that you cause him to lean forward. Finding his balance disturbed towards his right front corner he advances his right foot and tries to preserve his natural posture. Your retort is to entrust the weight of your body to your right leg, then to straighten your left leg and apply the sole of the foot to your opponent's right leg about midway between his knee and ankle, while at the same time, as with this movement you obstruct the further advance of his right leg, you bend backwards and twist the upper part of your body towards your left back corner. With both hands holding your opponent's left lapel and right sleeve respectively, you should maintain a progressively strengthening pull towards your torso. If these several movements have been successfully co-ordinated your opponent's balance will be broken more and more towards his right front corner until finally he falls to the mat. (Fig. 53).

Sasae-Tsurikomi-Ashi (*Propping Drawing Ankle Throw*)

This trip is best applied when your opponent is posed on the toes of one foot with his body rather stiff and upright. It is less effective against an opponent who stands loosely with a tendency to bend or lean backwards. Move your body to the right and place your right toes outside your opponent's left foot but less deeply than in the case of the Tsurikomi-Ashi. Use your right toes as fulcrum or pivot and turn your body to your left back but with a larger circular movement than in the first instance. Also the point of impact of your left sole is directly outside your opponent's right ankle and not midway between knee and ankle as in the case of the orthodox Tsurikomi-Ashi. Your aim is to pull your opponent continuously towards his right front corner until he has no more room to escape; in this manner you disturb and eventually break his balance (Kuzushi and Tsukuri) until he falls. As usual, synchronize the pull and lift on your opponent's sleeve and lapel with the pressure of your left sole against your opponent's right ankle. Fig. 53 (A)).

Kosotogari (*Minor Exterior Reaping Ankle Throw*)

It may happen that when engaged in the right natural posture you try to pull your opponent towards his right front

Fig. 53

Fig. 53 (A)

Fig. 54

Fig. 55

corner, when fearing that his balance may be disturbed or even broken in that direction he advances his right foot comparatively more to the front with the weight of his body resting rather upon the heel than the toes of that foot. This stance affords the most favourable opportunity for recourse to the Kosotogari, especially when as he withdraws his hips and waist to the rear the weight of his body tends to rest upon the back of the heel of his right foot. Now assuming a stand with your right foot pointing towards his right foot but at a convenient distance from its toes, your body held upright and supported by your right leg, bend back the big toe of your left foot in the semblance of a sickle and while your left foot rubs against the mat hook or "reap", as it were, the back heel of your opponent's right foot and at the same time pull him towards you. In this movement your left hand holding his right sleeve and your right hand grasping his left lapel must help the attack made with the " sickle " of your left foot until his balance is finally broken towards his right back corner and he falls. (Fig. 54).

The Kosotogari can also be applied when your opponent tends to move backwards. Say he attempts to pull you and to retreat or being pushed by you falls back a little. First of all he may draw back his left leg with the weight of his body still resting on his right leg; then while you are being pulled or while you are pushing, tilt him towards his right back corner, advance your right foot as before and " reap " his right back heel with the " sickle " of your left foot. Effectively executed the Kosotogari can be quite a heavy throw.

Kouchigari (Minor Interior Reaping Ankle Throw)

The most appropriate moment for attempting the Kouchigari, if you are engaged in the right natural posture, is when your opponent has advanced his left leg a little more than usual and his left foot is on the point of touching the ground but has not yet quite done so, and when the weight of his body is about to be transferred to that leg but before the process is complete. The appropriate Kuzushi or preliminary disturbance of the balance is as follows : First of all pull him in the direction of his right front corner when in an effort to maintain his natural posture he may advance about as far as he has been pulled. If so suddenly pull him towards his left front corner. This move often provides the most effective stance for Tsukuri and final Kaké involving the complete breaking of your opponent's balance and his downfall. The application of the inner reaping movement is as follows : Support your weight upon your right foot and apply the instep of your left foot to the inner side of your opponent's left heel in the semblance of a sickle sweeping it in the direction of its advance. Simultaneously with both hands assist this movement until your opponent finally loses his balance and falls. (Fig. 55).

Several important factors should not be lost sight of in practising this throw. Remember that once your opponent has actually planted his left foot on the ground and has completed the transfer of his weight to that leg, excessive strength would be required to bring off the throw. Again, sometimes your opponent may contrive to shift his stance and expose you to the danger of a counter technique. You must therefore be on the alert not to miss the most suitable moment for recourse to the Kouchigari. Nor is it sufficient to confine the " dynamic " of the reaping action to the instep of the attacking foot; as in virtually all Judo throws your entire bodily force, including the action of your hips and loins, must be called into play to ensure the perfect execution of this throw.

Need I again remind you that it is equally possible for you to " reap " your opponent's right foot from the inside with the inner edge or instep of your right foot? To do so naturally necessitates corresponding adjustments of stance.

The best and perhaps only way to escape the Kouchigari is to lift the threatened foot rapidly before it is swept and just before your opponent has " enveloped " it.

Harai-Tsurikomi-Ashi (Sweeping Drawing Ankle Throw)

There is a strong family resemblance between the Sasae-Tsurikomi-Ashi (Propping Drawing Ankle Throw) and the Harai-Tsurikomi-Ashi now to be described. There is very little difference, for example, between your own posture (shisei) and your applied Tsukuri or method of destroying your opponent's balance. In the orthodox method, when you are engaged in the right natural posture, this technique presupposes an attack with your left foot against your opponent's right leg in the region of his outer ankle bone. Watch for an opportunity when he is about to shift his weight on to his right foot but before he has actually done so and then sweep that foot with your left foot in an obliquely back direction and throw him. O-Cho-

Yoshio, 8th Dan of the Kodokan, adds the following details as recorded in the French " International Judo ", already quoted. The movements of the hands are important, but those of the whole body are even more so, above all those of the hips. The hand movements first. When your opponent is about to place his right foot on the mat turn your right hand slightly inwards, pull forward and to the right, your left forearm pressing against his chest backwards and to the left. Your weight is on the right foot which is outside his left foot, your toes slightly turned inwards. Your left leg is held very straight, the foot turned slightly inwards; then direct all your power towards your little toe and the ball of the foot nearest the joint of the big toe and sweep to your opponent's right rear corner pressing against the bottom of his instep. These movements are almost simultaneous. When you are both in the right natural posture but he advances his left foot, compel him to place it somewhere to the inside with the help of your right hand and pull with your left hand parallel to the mat so as to bring him on to his toes on both feet. Break his balance to the left front corner. When he moves his left foot forward place your right foot slightly in front of his left foot with your toes turned slightly inwards. In this case your left foot becomes straight and in line with your body from the toes to the head like a stick and you sweep the base of his right instep. At this instant your left hand, which has been pulling parallel to the ground to the front, changes direction and pulls downwards to the rear left corner very swiftly and you throw.

When you are in front of an opponent in the extreme of the natural posture and you wish to apply this throw with your right foot, first change your posture to the left natural posture by moving your right foot; you disturb his balance by lifting him a bit; move your left foot to the inside of his right foot and sweep his *left* foot with the inside of your *right* foot. (Fig. 56 illustrates the latter method).

INSTRUCTION V

SELECTION OF THROWS EFFECTED IN A LYING POSITION

Sutemiwaza

I NOW come to the fourth and final branch of the Nagewaza or throwing methods. The throws included in this category of Sutemiwaza, sometimes called "sacrifice" throws or "abandonment technique", require you when executing them to fall yourself with your back or your side on the ground. The word itself is derived from the verbal stem of " suteru " meaning to throw away, abandon, discard, etc. and "waza" technique. The " u " in sutemi is a short vowel and so slurred as to be scarcely audible. Thus the word is pronounced almost as if written " stemiwaza ".

The technique of the sub-division in which you fall with your back on the ground in order to apply the throw is styled " Masutemiwaza " and that of the sub-division in which you fall with your side on the ground in order to apply the throw is styled " Yokosutemiwaza ".

Since the execution of these throws makes comparatively less demand upon the performer's physical strength and bodily suppleness than does that of the throws from a standing position (Tachiwaza) already described, they are often favoured by older judoka who find it advisable to conserve their energies. At the same time, I think that after studying and testing for yourself the throws I shall try to describe under this head, you will agree with me that in a real fight their successful application might come as a nasty surprise to an unscrupulous aggressor.

MASUTEMIWAZA

Tomoenage (Throwing in a Circle or Whirling Throw, often called the Stomach Throw)

It is possible that you already know something about this throw from casual demonstrations or displays to which it lends itself quite effectively. And although I myself do not rank it among Judo methods characterized by " general elegance ", it cannot be doubted that when thoroughly mastered by the pupil it may be practically applied to good purpose in a genuine rough and tumble. Indeed I remember even now how on more than one occasion a hefty English or American bluejacket looking for trouble in the old Yokohama " Bloodtown " of unsavoury reputation managed to find it at the hands and feet of a comparatively small Japanese policeman who hurled him through space with precisely this Tomoenage.

Let us assume, as before, that you are engaged in the right natural posture. Relinquish your left-hand hold on your opponent's right sleeve and with both hands grasp his left and right side collar in the normal grip already explained. Masking your true design, push strongly against him as though trying to disturb his balance towards his direct rear. Now if he seeks to defend himself by pushing you in return, slip your left leg between both his legs and utilize his strength exerted in pushing you back in order to make him lose his balance towards his direct front; then retaining your firm hand grip on your opponent's lapels slide to the ground with your buttocks as far forward as possible and the heel of your left foot lowered to your direct rear. At the same time bend your right leg and apply the sole very lightly to your opponent's lower abdomen. Still without in any way relaxing your hold on his lapels throw yourself backwards breaking his balance more and more. At this point straighten your bent right leg the sole of whose foot has been applied to his lower abdomen and the propulsive force of this movement should suffice to send him flying over your head to the mats beyond, describing an arc in its flight through space. (Fig. 57).

Although in this technique your opponent is thrown by the combined action of your hands drawing the upper part of his body downwards and the propulsive force of your foot operating reciprocally in opposition to each other, yet if the propulsive force of your foot is inadequate you may very well fail to bring off this throw. It is therefore advisable that when you lower your buttocks you should conserve the propulsive force of your bent right leg. It is also essential that as they touch the mats your buttocks should be as far forward as possible. If they are not, then your right leg being automatically extended at the start of the movement cannot be so conveniently bent and, of course, subsequently straightened to send

Fig. 56

Fig. 57

Fig. 58

Fig. 59

JAK

your opponent flying over your head. Your aim must therefore be to synchronize the several movements involved to the best advantage, i.e. lowering of buttocks, raising of right foot, contact of buttocks with the mat, application of the sole of right foot to opponent's lower abdomen, etc. Be careful not to use undue force when applying the sole of your foot to your opponent's stomach, otherwise you may injure him. It is therefore a good plan to curve the toes backward and apply approximately the forepart of the sole to your opponent's stomach a little below the navel. It goes without saying that in a real scrap you would be far less scrupulous about the force employed with your right foot to hurl your victim over your head to the ground beyond.

Uranage (Rear Throw)

There are two ways of executing this throw. In the first and older version the assailant threw his opponent from behind, whereas in the later version he takes a frontal hold. In my humble opinion the older version is much to be preferred to the newer one and its execution is besides more in consonance with its name of " Rear Throw ". I therefore make no apology for describing it here in somewhat greater detail than the newer version, after which I shall devote a paragraph to the latter for purposes of reference and comparison.

A blow aimed at your head by your opponent with his right fist can provide an opening for this throw. To dodge the blow you may shift the upper part of your body obliquely to the left, and your opponent being carried forward by the momentum of the blow may involuntarily tend to turn slightly to the left on his right foot until finally his balance is impaired towards his right back corner. Taking advantage of the opportunity slip behind his right back corner and lowering your waist embrace your opponent with your arms in the following manner : Bring your chest into the closest possible contact with the region of his waist, your left arm extended from his rear along his belt so that the palm of the hand is applied to the lower part of his side at his left front corner and your right to the front corner of his lower abdomen and slightly pointing upwards, and in this stance clasp him firmly to your left breast. To throw him you should bend backwards. Then as with both your arms you exert a lifting pressing movement in the direction of your left shoulder and using also the strength of your body, you lift your opponent so that his feet are separated from the mat. Now lower your body somewhat, throw yourself backwards and hurl your opponent over your shoulder to your direct rear. This is a genuine rear throw. (Fig. 58).

In the later version, when your opponent aims a blow at you with his right fist, you advance your left foot to the outside and slightly behind your opponent's right foot. Then place your left hand, which passes behind your opponent's back, on his left hip and simultaneously place your right hand behind his back as far as his right hip. Now advance your right foot in front of your opponent's feet with the left side of your head placed in front of his chest. Your opponent is thus thrown off balance as you lift him from the mat and let yourself fall and propel your opponent over your left shoulder. If the throw has been correctly applied with sufficient momentum, your opponent should turn over in the air and land on his back.

It may be advisable for you to practise both these methods so as to be prepared to take advantage of either opening.

Sumigaeshi (Corner Throw)

In contradistinction to most of the throws hitherto described, the Sumigaeshi is applied from the self-defensive instead of the natural posture, i.e. with both knees and torso bent and lowered. You thread your right arm under your opponent's left armpit so that hand and arm are applied as far as possible to the upper part of the left rear corner of his back, and your left hand grasps his inside right sleeve from the elbow in the region of the forearm in the normal grip. Alternatively you can pin his right arm snugly against your left armpit and with your right hand hold his left front belt at the side also in the normal grip. To get your opponent off balance you alternately pull and push him and if you succeed in making him advance his right foot, while his left foot is raised in a buoyant state, the moment is opportune for attempting the Sumigaeshi. Maintaining maximum contact between your two bodies, advance your left foot to the outside of your opponent's right foot, lower your buttocks to the front, apply the shin of your right leg to your opponent's left inner rear thigh, and throw yourself to your direct rear; simultaneously with your right leg fling up your opponent's left thigh in the direction of its rise. Concurrently with your left hand pull your opponent's body downwards and with your right hand push and lift it. If these moves have been properly co-ordinated your opponent should land from the tip of his right shoulder obliquely on to his back. (Fig. 59).

An important point to be observed in connexion with this technique is that if when the weight of your opponent's body is resting on his right leg he happens to be holding himself loosely, even though you fling up his left inner thigh with the shin of your inserted right leg as you lie on the ground, yet by keeping it buoyant and putting no strength into it he may very well nullify your effort to complete the throw. Consequently the most favourable opportunity for utilizing his broken balance is when his body is being held somewhat stiffly.

Yokosutemiwaza

The rest of the throws in this section belong to the sub-division of Yokosutemiwaza or throws effected with one's side on the ground. The first on my list is the so-called

Ukiwaza (Floating Throw)

This throw has been rightly described as one for advanced judoka and since it is also a throw that could be very effectively used in a serious struggle I propose to deal with it at some length. Thus first I shall describe it as demonstrated in the pre-arranged Nage-no-Kata or Forms of Throwing and then on the basis of valuable data supplied by Yamaguchi Magosaku, 8th Dan of the Kodokan, quoted in the French publication " International Judo " (Kokusai Judo).

It is assumed that you are engaged in the right self-defensive posture, each holding the other with the right part of the body forward. You should hold your opponent's left side collar or lapel with your right hand in the normal grip or alternatively with your right arm threaded under his left armpit so that your hand is applied to the upper part of the left rear corner of his back. In this stance you first pull him to his right, then to his left, then a second time to his right, when he tends to lose balance towards his right front corner. When the weight of his body is poised more or less on the little toe of his right foot, advance your left foot deeply to the outside of his right foot. and block its further advance with that foot. Simultaneously bending backwards abandon yourself to the rear throwing your opponent with your bodily momentum. You fall yourself with your left rear corner coming in contact with the mat. It should

Fig. 60

Fig. 61

Fig. 62

Fig. 63

JAK

be noted that not only in this method but generally in all Yokosutemiwaza your body lands with its rear corner on the mat while your thrown opponent's body and your own lie almost side by side, whereas in the case of the Masutemiwaza the direction of your own fall is the direct rear in which your two bodies form almost a straight line.

In his description of this throw Yamaguchi Magosaku remarks that on approaching your opponent the latter may move his right foot forward. You then move back a large pace with your right foot behind you, pulling him and breaking his balance to the front left corner. He may move his left foot forward to keep his balance. At that very moment you should lift him slightly and so induce him to move his right foot naturally forward to the right front corner. You should then break his balance in the same direction; stretch your left leg, which you open widely to the left, and abandon your body to the left throwing your opponent in the direction of your left shoulder. Your right hand inserted under his left armpit should be held like a spoon with all your strength in your little finger. Whether you apply this throw to left or right, the direction in which you break your opponent's balance should be the same as that in which you abandon your body, both moving in the same direction like a rolling wheel or arc. Make good use of your hands to lift him slightly in helping to break his balance just before you stretch out your left leg, open it widely, abandon your body on to the left side and throw him in the direction of your left shoulder. (Fig. 60).

Yokogake (Side Body Drop)

It is again assumed that you are engaged in the right natural posture, and as in the case of Ukiotoshi, while preserving your natural posture you retreat a pace or two and drawing your opponent in your wake try to disturb his balance towards his right front corner. In his turn your opponent advancing as far as he has been pulled tries to retain his natural posture. But at the third step you should bend back a little and pull him more than expected so that his body like a stick unbalanced towards his right front corner is tilted vertically in that direction with his weight resting almost on the little toe of his right foot. At this juncture you should support your entire body on your right leg and with the sole of your left foot sweep the outer ankle bone of your opponent's right foot, while simultaneously holding your body like a stick you fall to your rear bringing your opponent with you. In falling your left back corner comes in contact with the mat but your right back corner does not. As in nearly all Judo throws operation of the hands is all important. So with the Yokogake the momentum of your own voluntary fall and of the throw executed against your opponent is intensified by the pull which you give in the direction of your body with your left hand holding your opponent's right sleeve, and the lift-pull (tsurikomi) imparted by your right hand grasping your opponent's left lapel. If the technique has been correctly executed your opponent should land on his back. (Fig. 61).

In practising this throw you should be careful to avoid undue violence. If for instance at the moment when with both hands you are pulling your opponent you drag him directly downwards, he may be thrown very heavily, and there is a risk of injuring his shoulder. Thus an inexperienced pupil is well advised to exercise caution in this respect. If the Yokogake has been correctly done your opponent should not fall far away from you, and his body should lie almost parallel with your own.

Yokoguruma (Side Wheel)

As in the case of the Uranage already described, the Yokoguruma can be attempted in retort to a blow aimed at your head by your opponent. You dodge the blow with a quick body shift to your left. Your opponent's turn to his right back corner, his posture and the way he applies both hands, etc., are exactly the same as in the Uranage. However, should you try to apply the Uranage your opponent may thwart your purpose by bending his body to the front. Instead you should from the front insert your right leg deeply between your opponent's thighs and utilizing the momentum of his forward bend twist your body somewhat to the left and drop to the mat. Simultaneously synchronizing the operation of your left hand with the movement of your body, you pull and turn your opponent, and with the added help of your right hand throw him in the direction of the side of your left shoulder. (Fig. 62).

Yoko-otoshi (Side Drop)

Say you are engaged in the right self-defensive posture, i.e., with somewhat bent knees and lowered waist, your right arm thrust under your opponent's left armpit, your left hand hugging his forearm from the elbow on the outside. If in this position you pull him alternately to his left and right front corner, he may sometimes have his weight resting on his right leg. Now you must pull him more and more towards his right front corner; then with the upper inside edge of your left ankle you should rub against the region of the outer ankle of your opponent's right foot and in that manner block the further progress of that leg, while simultaneously retaining your hold on his right forearm you abandon your body to your left back corner. Both your hands help to draw your opponent to your body until he is, as it were, dropped towards his right front corner. As you abandon yourself you turn your body slightly so that your left rear corner comes in contact with the mat. Your opponent's fallen body and your own come to rest almost parallel with each other. (Fig. 63).

In the execution of this throw the manner of clasping your opponent is highly important. If when so doing you loosen your arm hold on your opponent he will run the risk of injuring his shoulder. Again, since your opponent is thrown by the momentum of your falling body, if in the course of the throw you relax your arm hold, the efficacy of your technique will be impaired. Therefore until the very end of the throw be careful not to loosen your hold.

Yokowakare (Side Separation)

This throw may be called a companion throw to the Yokogake already described. You are engaged in the right natural posture; your hand hold is the same as with the Yokogake; the Tsukuri or destruction of your opponent's balance is also much the same. As he is pulled your opponent keeps pace with you and advances with the weight of his body resting on his right leg, and his balance being imperilled towards his right front corner he may be tilted forward. In that case you should throw out both your legs to his right side, the upper half of your body turned slightly to your left, and as you let yourself fall in this position your opponent should be thrown towards his right front corner. (Fig. 64).

It should be pointed out that although there may seem to be quite a family resemblance among the three throws, Yokogake, Yokowakare and Yoko-otoshi, there are none the less certain details in which they differ from one another. The more important are cited below.

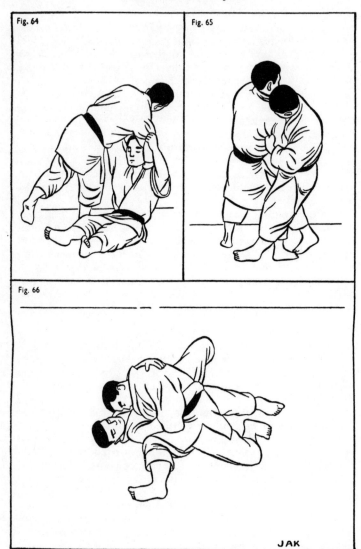

Fig. 64

Fig. 65

Fig. 66

JAK

As regards the manner in which the two contestants engage each other : In the case of the Yokogake and Yokowakare they may do so in either the right or left natural posture, whereas in the case of the Yoko-otoshi they are engaged in the right or left self-defensive posture. Then as regards the Kuzushi or method of disturbing opponent's posture or balance, in most instances the assailant, when attempting the Yokogake and Yokowakare, pulls his opponent continuously towards either the latter's right or left front corner, whereas when attempting the Yoko-otoshi he pulls his opponent alternately towards the latter's left and right front corner. Then when we come to the method of Kake or actual execution of the throw, when attempting the Yokogake the assailant sweeps the upper part of his opponent's outer ankle with the sole of his foot, whereas when attempting the Yoko-otoshi he does not sweep his opponent's foot with his foot but only advances his foot so as to prevent the further progress of the foot on which his opponent's balance has already been disrupted. However, in the case of the Yokowakare, although the assailant does not sweep his opponent's foot with his foot, as in the case of the Yokogake, or as in the case of the Yoko-otoshi advance one foot, the tempo of the disturbance of the opponent's balance is sustained until the moment when the assailant thrusts out both legs in falling to throw his opponent. Besides the foregoing, there are other subtle differences in the manner of disturbing balance (Kuzushi) and of effecting the actual throw (Kake), but for most practical purposes emphasis on the foregoing three points will suffice.

Tani-otoshi (Valley Drop)

As in the case of the Yoko-otoshi, when applying the Tani-otoshi you are engaged in the right self-defensive posture. You make a feint to break his balance towards his right front corner, when he may quite likely oppose this move either by drawing back or by attempting to disturb your balance towards your right front corner, when his weight may rest on his right leg and his left foot may be pulled back. Then he may begin to withdraw his body together with his right leg and while his weight is not yet wholly removed from that leg his balance may tend to be disturbed towards his right back corner or if for any other reason his natural posture is broken in that direction you can advantageously attempt the Tani-otoshi. Advance your left leg in such wise that it is applied downwards with a scraping movement from the upper part of the right back corner of your opponent's right shin. Simultaneously abandon the upper half of your body to your left front corner while with your right arm threaded under your opponent's left armpit you lift and push him slightly and with the combined force of your left arm hugging his right sleeve and your body you drop him towards his right back corner. (Fig. 65).

The points in which the Tani-otoshi differs from the Yoko-otoshi can be epitomized as follows : In the first place, in the Yoko-otoshi your body falls to your back corner, whereas in the Tani-otoshi it falls to your front corner. In the second place, in the Yoko-otoshi your opponent's body falls to his front corner, whereas in the Tani-otoshi it falls to his rear corner. Thirdly, whereas in the execution of the Yoko-otoshi it is essential at the time of both Tsukuri and Kake until the completion of the technique to retain your clutch with one hand on your opponent's sleeve, in the execution of the Tani-otoshi retention of your hold is necessary at the time of Tsukuri but not so necessary at the time of Kake.

Before passing on in my next lesson to a description of Katamewaza or Groundwork, I should again impress upon you the advisability of familiarizing yourself thoroughly with the meaning of the Japanese Judo terminology given in the glossary appended to my first lesson. More especially should you master the meaning of the important terms Kuzushi—disturbing balance, Tsukuri—destroying balance, and Kake—the actual throwing. The late Dr. Jigoro Kano, the great creator of Judo and founder of the Kodokan, defined Tsukuri and Kake respectively as " fitting action for attack " and " attack ". The words are different but their implication is the same. One does not need to be unduly pedantic in the use of these terms; it is far more to the purpose that one's mind should be clear as to their technical significance when applied to specific techniques.

INSTRUCTION VI

KATAMEWAZA OR GROUNDWORK—SELECTED HOLD-DOWNS OR OSAEKOMIWAZA

ETYMOLOGICALLY the Japanese term Katamewaza is composed of two ideographs, the first " Katame " meaning literally "hardening " and " defence " and the second " waza " meaning literally " act ", " deed ", " work ", " art ", " trick ", " technique ", etc. It is classified into three sub-divisions, viz., (1) Osaekomiwaza or Hold-downs; (2) Shimewaza (sometimes called Shibori) or Chokelocks and Strangleholds otherwise Necklocks, and (3) Kansetsuwaza or Gyaku, meaning Bonelocks. An overall name Newaza is usually applied to this branch as a whole.

Although doubtless Katamewaza lacks the spectacular attributes of Tachiwaza or tricks executed in a standing position, and perhaps for that reason has been to some extent relegated to a secondary place even at the famous Kodokan of Tokyo, there has latterly been in international Judo circles a steadily growing recognition of its great importance which, in my opinion, can hardly be exaggerated. I can quite well imagine a situation in which, if one were up against an exceptionally tough antagonist, even a heavy throw might fail to prove conclusive. Or again, if one were involved in a life-and-death struggle within a confined space, a railway compartment, for example, there would be no room to apply a standing throw. In such a situation one's ignorance of Katamewaza might easily lead to one's ignominious defeat and knock-out, if not necessarily death, whereas if one were thoroughly well versed in the numerous methods of Katamewaza, one would stand a far better chance of overpowering one's adversary and rendering him helpless until official help arrived, even without being forced to proceed to the extremity of killing him, as one could easily do. The justification for this confidence will appear from the fact that apart from the necessarily painful methods of chokelocks, strangleholds and bonelocks included in the sub-divisions of Shimewaza and Kansetsuwaza, one has the choice

111

of hold-downs or Osaekomiwaza whereby one's adversary can be immobilized for an indefinite period, if one's victim is ignorant of the art, without excessive strain on one's own part.

And admitting that during early stages of training, practice in groundwork inevitably imposes quite a severe demand upon the pupil's strength and endurance, the fact that it is on the whole attended by less danger of injury than Tachiwaza, wherein a clumsy fall may sometimes result in a broken bone, will recommend it to older judoka who are not quite so nippy on their pins as they used to be. Apart from these mundane considerations, groundwork is a splendid physical exercise and brings into play muscles and sinews not always reached in Tachiwaza.

Although reluctant to inflict upon you an overdose of theory, I think you can profitably devote some attention to a brief exposition of rationale and basic principles. In Osaekomiwaza or hold-downs, the spot to which your strength must be applied is generally your opponent's body. For the moment therefore let us liken his body to a rectangular board lying on the ground. If you wanted to lift this rectangular board your simplest plan would be to raise one of its corners. And conversely, if you wanted to prevent the board from rising, your simplest course would be to push down the corner trying to rise. Now substituting a human being for a rectangular board, if you want to prevent a prostrate opponent from getting up, you must, according to circumstances, bring your waist, hips, loins and shoulders to bear with the appropriate amount of strength against the point at which your opponent is trying to rise, e.g., shoulder or hip for the most part. But when you bring strength to bear against the direction in which your opponent is trying to get up, as likely as not he will suddenly try to get up from an angle against which your strength has not been directed ! From what has been said it will be realized that in these hold-downs or Osaekomiwaza, everything depends upon a combination of quick thinking, correct timing, agility, patience and endurance. It is therefore essential that, on the one hand, the person being held down should endeavour as far as possible to detect the points where his assailant's strength is lacking while, on the other, the assailant who is uppermost and is trying to hold him down should constantly manipulate his position so that such vulnerable points of weakness are not available and so that he is ready on the instant to bring pressure to bear against any corner from which his opponent is trying to get up. In this context I cannot do better than quote some pertinent remarks made by Tsunetani Oda, 9th Dan of the Kodokan, from a translation appearing in the current issue of the French publication " International Judo " (Kokusai Judo) :

" Keep down the shoulder or hip which is trying to raise itself and control the points of contact such as the elbows and the knees. He who is underneath should try with all his might to find openings; he who is on top, for his part, should take care that they do not appear. When first applying a hold-down, do not be too relaxed or too tensed up or too occupied with what you are doing, but keep an eye on the position of your body and be completely relaxed when your opponent tries to counter attack by lifting you up. Defend yourself with your forehead, hands, feet and shoulders as supports, and escape by turning around in order to apply another sort of hold down. For young people Katamewaza is considered uninteresting, but nevertheless there are many interesting points in Osaekomiwaza which do not appear in Nagewaza. Besides Newaza has more variations and is less dangerous than Nagewaza, and in a short time one makes much more progress. It also cultivates a spirit of patience which is very important in real life."

When to the comparatively painless techniques of Osaekomiwaza or hold-downs are added the potentially deadly chokelocks and strangleholds afforded by the Shimewaza or Shibori sub-division and the potentially painful and crippling methods of Kansetsuwaza or bonelocks, no reasonable judoka need have cause for complaint about the tameness or lack of variety of the Katamewaza repertoire !

Mindful of the danger latent in the two last sub-divisions, the late Sakujiro Yokoyama, one of the greatest Judo masters of all time, in his book on the art, a copy of which he bequeathed to me many years ago, urges that for insufficiently experienced pupils the most advisable sequence of training would be from Nagewaza to Osaekomiwaza and then gradually to Shimewaza and Kansetsuwaza.

The first hold-down I shall try to describe for you here is called

Kesagatame or Hongesa (Scarf Hold or Lock)

As in practically all Judo techniques so in the domain of groundwork all holds can be applied from both the right and left side of one's opponent. And adhering to the generally accepted practice I shall confine myself to an explanation of the right side approach. Any intelligent pupil, once apprised of the right side approach, should be fully competent to convert it into a left side approach when the respective postures of himself and his opponent make such variants advisable.

Assuming then that you are kneeling on the right side of your recumbent opponent you must swiftly change your posture so that you are reclining against and facing him with your right waist touching your opponent's right waist, and the closest contact established between your two bodies obliquely from your opponent's abdominal region to his left breast. Your right arm should be thrust from under his left armpit so that the hand grasps his left shoulder, and your left hand should hold his right sleeve as deeply as possible from the outside so that his right arm is firmly hugged against your left side. Your breast should press heavily down upon the upper part of your opponent's chest. Your right knee should be bent and the thigh applied as snugly as possible to his right flank. Your left leg should also be bent and stretched out to your rear touching the mat. Now if your opponent tries to get up by raising, say, his right shoulder, you must thwart his attempt with the pressure and control of your chest and left arm. Again, if he tries to pull you over his body from right to left, you should let go your right arm hold on his left arm and prop yourself with your hand placed on the mat on that side, controlling him with the co-ordinated operation of your hips and both legs. Again, should he, while twisting his waist to the left withdraw his body and try to shift you to the rear and get up, you must uninterruptedly advance your waist and both legs maintaining unbroken contact so that no open space is left between your two bodies to facilitate his efforts to shake you off with this manœuvre. Supplementing these counter measures with the control exercised by your left arm and chest, you may succeed in baulking all his efforts to get up. (Fig. 66).

Fusegi or Defence Technique. There are several possible defences against the foregoing form of hold-down, but I shall content myself with describing two methods which seem to me most likely to be effective. As a general principle your movements should be directed to disruption of the relative positions of your assailant's body and your own, which are, so to say, a prerequisite for a successful hold-down, and to releasing yourself from your assailant's control rather than to merely local defence or attack.

Assuming that you are being held with a Kesagatame applied on your right side, that the hold has been rigidly applied, and that your assailant's body is stiffened, grip his belt at the back with your left hand and push him upward, straightening your arm as you bridge your body and turn slightly to your right in such a way as to tip him forward on to his face. Then holding him up with your hand, slide your body under him. This move will almost balance him on your abdomen or bring your abdomen into contact with his buttock. Retaining a firm hold and bridging your body, turn over to your left, landing your assailant on your left side.

A second method may offer itself when your assailant neglects his legs and brings them close together. Push him upward with both your hands, arms straightened; simultaneously bridge your body, tilting your assailant towards your face. Then on recoil of the movement roll forward with the action of a rocking-horse so as to get your assailant on the mat underneath your body. Be careful not to relax the pushing movement as you roll.

It goes without saying that there are counter moves to these defences, but an attempt to describe them all in detail would tend only to confuse you and would besides expand this course far beyond the limits set for it.

Kuzurekesagatame (Broken Scarf Hold)

Engaged with your opponent in the Hongesa position already described you substitute for your right-hand hold enfolding his neck from his left side a hold in which your right hand may either be threaded through his left armpit to grip his right-side collar or else spread with the palm on the mat between your opponent's left arm and left flank. (Fig. 66 (A).)

Fusegi or Defence Technique : Bring the heels of both your legs close to your buttocks, swing your body, twist your hips to the right; clench the fist of your left hand and insert it under your opponent's throat. Simultaneously stretch both legs and extricate your right arm. When your opponent to prevent the withdrawal of your right arm pushes with his body, hug his right arm against your left flank; with your right hand seize the region of his front belt, switch your body in the opposite direction to the left and overturn him towards the back of your

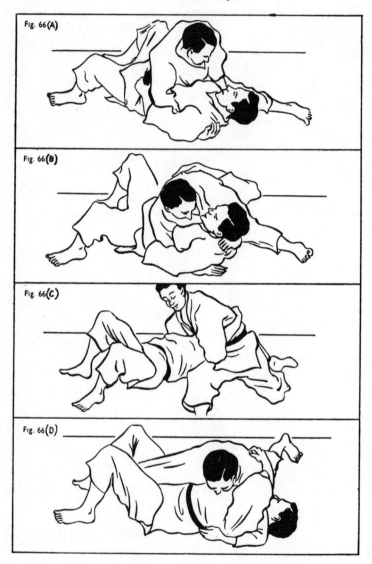

Fig. 66(A)

Fig. 66(B)

Fig. 66(C)

Fig. 66(D)

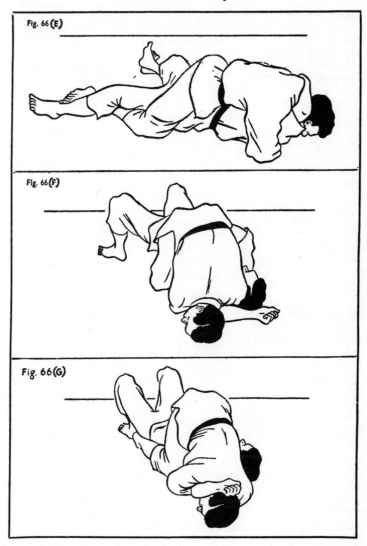

Fig. 66 (E)

Fig. 66 (F)

Fig. 66 (G)

left shoulder. If in defence against this manoeuvre your opponent twists his body to the left and pushing with his right hand places it on the mat, insert your left hand from underneath and pushing it above his head remove it. At the same time twist your body to the right so as to establish contact with his back, and extricating your right arm escape from the holding.

An effective continuation technique or Renrakuwaza stemming from the foregoing method is thus described : If your opponent has contrived to extricate his right arm from under your left armpit, instantly pass your left arm under his neck and seize his back collar near his left shoulder with your thumb inside and carry on the immobilization as before. (Fig. 66 (B).)

Ushirokesagatame (Rear Scarf Hold)

This method is applied with your back turned towards your supine opponent's head, as shown in Fig. 66 (C), as you attack him from his left side. With your left arm you enfold his left arm and pin it tightly under your left armpit while at the same time with your right elbow you press strongly against his right upper arm.

Katagatame (Shoulder Holding or Shoulder Lock)

This is an appreciably more drastic hold-down than the foregoing and pregnant with belligerent possibilities. There are two variations of this hold-down both of which I shall try to describe below.

In the first method the manner of adjusting waist, hips and legs is just the same as in the Kesagatame. Assuming as before that you are attacking your opponent from his right side, your right arm must be passed from over the tip of his left shoulder under his neck. Then your left arm must be threaded from under the tip of his right shoulder until both your right and left hands meet and clasp each other. Now the rôle played by your head is vitally important. Its right side should press strongly against the upper part of the right side of your opponent's head in such a way that his right upper arm is locked between the right side of your neck and his face. With the sustained pressure of the right side of your head and neck you force his right arm well over to his left so that it is firmly pinned or locked and rendered helpless. (Fig. 67).

Fig. 67

Fig. 68

Fig. 69

In the second method of Katagatame, although the grip with both your hands and the manner of controlling the free movement of your opponent's upper right arm are identical with the first-named method, the disposal of your legs is quite different. Thus you should bend your right knee as if you were going to squat, the shin touching the mat, while you maintain the maximum contact with your opponent's right side, your buttocks uppermost and your left leg extended to your left side. From this position your opponent's efforts to rise should be opposed as in the first method.

If you are inclined to debase the Katagatame into a species of " rough house " lock designed to inflict acute discomfort if not disablement upon your opponent, see that your left hand passed under the tip of his right shoulder to meet your right hand passed from over the tip of his left shoulder under his neck, clasps your right hand so that the latter hand is, as it were, cupped in the palm of your left hand held upwards, with fingers normally overlapping the little finger edge of the right hand in a firm grip. In this hold the sharp wrist bone of the thumb edge of your right hand can be held against your opponent's jugular vein and carotid artery, and the maximum leftward pull of your left hand on your right hand may exert such pressure at these vulnerable points as to menace him with unconsciousness, if nothing worse.

If you are applying the Katagatame from your opponent's left side, you have merely to reverse this hold so that your left hand is cupped in your right hand palm, the sharp thumb edge of your left wrist held against your opponent's carotid artery, when with the maximum *rightward* pull of your right hand on your left hand you may similarly exert such pressure as to reduce your opponent to insensibility.

Defence against Katagatame : As before assume that you are being held down on your right-hand side. Contracting the muscles of the shoulders and neck resist your assailant's pressure on your right arm and shoulder; wriggle to the right and left in quick succession to confuse your assailant and make him misdirect his pressure on you or change his position. If your assailant switches his pressure towards your face, turn your right shoulder quickly to your left. This move will not free you but will break the holding and open a way for escape. As you turn your shoulder, force your right arm down against your assailant's right arm, then drawing your right elbow to your side turn your body sharply to your right to face your assailant. Simultaneously draw up your right knee and press it against your assailant. These several actions should be carried out in swift succession to retain the initiative.

A second defence method presupposes the same initial actions as described above. When your assailant changes his pressure upward, utilizing his force turn your body over upward, pivoting on your head and shoulders so as to land yourself on the mat on your knees above your assailant's right shoulder. Then if your assailant does not draw his arm away attack him with an armlock. Otherwise you may be able to apply the Kamishihogatame or Upper Four Quarters which I shall next describe.

Kamishihogatame (Locking of Upper Four Quarters)

In this hold-down you take up a kneeling position behind your prostrate opponent's head as he lies on his back. Your right hand is passed from under his right arm to grasp his right side belt in the normal grip; your left hand is similarly passed from under his left arm to grasp his left side belt. His head is beneath your stomach, and your head bears down approximately in the region of his midriff. Both your knees are opened and your waist is lowered to the utmost. Now if your opponent tries to rise from a shoulder, you must at once manipulate your torso so as to push that shoulder down. If he twists his hips and waist and makes a desperate effort to get up, control and restrain him with both hands. Similarly from whatever direction he seeks to rise you must apply the appropriate hold-down pressure. (Fig. 68).

Moreover, remember that even if your hand-holds and the manipulation of your body are on the whole good, yet if when you are directing your strength to one point only you allow yourself to become unduly absorbed and tensed up over the immediate problem confronting you, there is always a danger lest your opponent should take advantage of an opening at a spot where your strength is absent and manage to shake you off and get up. This sort of risk is not, of course, confined to this particular hold-down; it is always present in every branch of groundwork. What therefore you should always aim at achieving is a technique which will enable you to preserve your presence of mind and to avoid the strain of putting your strength ceaselessly into your entire body so that you can con-

serve your energy and always have a useful surplus upon
which to draw to counter your opponent's efforts, whatever
form they happen to take. The importance of this golden rule
can hardly be overrated.

Defence : Bridge your body and endeavour to turn it to your
right and left. While so doing find an opportunity to insert
your right arm between your assailant's head and your chest;
then press your arm against your assailant's head sideways and
in the form of a recoil revolve your body to your left so as to get
your head out of the cover of your assailant's body. This move
should bring your body in a position at right angles to your
assailant's. The holding is now broken and a way is open for
you to attack in your turn. Quickly bring up your right knee
against your opponent's left groin, push away his right leg with
your left foot and clamp his body between your legs in order to
have control over his movements. If you have an opportunity,
grip your opponent's collar at the back of his neck with your
right hand, fingers inside; with your left hand the collar at the
right side of his neck, the thumb inside. Then bending your
right arm over your right shoulder, bring the forearm into contact with the front of your opponent's throat and apply a necklock.

In another defence, turn your body to your right and draw
back your right shoulder with a jerk to extricate your right arm
from your assailant's hold, and with the freed hand grip your
opponent's belt at the front; with the left hand at the back.
Then pushing your assailant upward with your right hand,
pulling with the left, turn him over your body to land him to
your left.

Kuzure-Kamishihogatame (Broken Locking of
Upper Four Quarters)

This is a simple variant of the foregoing. It can sometimes
be applied if your opponent hoping to escape from the Kamishihogatame, manages to draw out one arm and thrusts it under
your right armpit. In that case you may advantageously from
above your opponent pass your right arm under his upper arm
and take a firm hold of his back collar. In all other respects the
rest of the technique is much the same as the Kamishihogatame.

Yokoshihogatame (Lateral Locking of Four Quarters)

It is assumed that you are applying this hold-down from
your opponent's right side, as usual. You take up a kneeling

position on the mat. Your right arm is passed from above between his legs and under his left thigh so as to secure a normal grip on his back belt. Your left arm is passed from his right shoulder under his neck to secure a regular grip of his back collar. You must keep your knees wide apart and in close contact with your opponent's right flank. His right hand is pinned between your left upper arm and your left upper thigh. Your breast is placed above his stomach. Now if your opponent in an attempt to get up moves to his left, you should follow him up in order not to permit contact between your knees and his side to be broken, while too with the help of your left arm and thigh you do everything in your power to prevent him from making use of his right arm. Similarly you must do your best to counter his efforts to get up by applying your strength of arms, knees and body to the point from which danger threatens. (Fig. 69).

Defence : If attacked with this hold-down from your right side, grip your assailant's belt at the front with your right hand and bridge your body as high as you can and at the same time push your assailant down towards your leg with the help of your left hand. Then by withdrawing your right hip turn your body to your right and raise your right knee against your assailant's abdomen. These movements should break the hold and open a way for counter attacks.

In another method, grip your assailant's belt, the front with your right hand and the back with your left. Then, pulling with the left and pushing with the right, turn your opponent over your body and land him on the mat.

Kuzureyokoshihogatame
(Broken Lateral Locking of Four Quarters)

Your opponent is as before lying on his back and you are attacking him from his right side. Your left hand is passed over his left shoulder so as to grip his left-side belt. Your left elbow is kept taut so as to control his head and shoulder. Your right hand is inserted between his thighs to take hold optionally of his back mid-belt or his trousers. Your right knee is placed against your opponent's right flank and your left leg stretched to the rear with both feet raised on the toes and your hips lowered. Strength should be infused into your lower abdomen and your chest expanded. (Fig. 66 (D).)

By way of continuation technique or Renrakuwaza from the

Kuzureyokoshihogatame you may sometimes detect an opening for recourse to the Tateshihogatame or Lengthwise Locking of the Four Quarters described further on. The *modus operandi* in that case is to relinquish your right hand grip on your opponent's trousers and thrust your right hand from under his left armpit so as to stretch his left arm upwards. Then you straddle his torso and apply the Tateshihogatame (q.v.). It goes without saying that your choice of Henka or change will be dictated largely by your opponent's efforts to escape.

Fusegi or Defence Technique sometimes called Nogare-Kata or Escape Methods : With your left hand seize your opponent's back belt and with your right hand his front belt. Swing your body to the right. Insert your right knee under his body, brace yourself strongly and you may escape. Or else insert your knee more and more deeply and contrive to get your opponent between your legs to break the holding. Or else insert your right hand from between your opponent's left arm and your own body and as you arch your body backwards to your left rear extricate your right arm and so loosen the holding. In the first two cases if your opponent presses heavily forward with his body utilize his momentum, twist your body to the left and you may succeed in capsizing him over your left shoulder.

Tateshihogatame
(Lengthwise Locking of Four Quarters)

I rate this method as among the more effective contest Osaekomiwaza and as such well worth study. It is assumed that your opponent is lying on his back and that you have straddled his torso equestrian fashion. Now pass your right hand underneath his left armpit and your left hand underneath his right armpit, and with your four fingers inside grip his back collar. Stretch both legs so that your right leg is thrust from the outside under your opponent's left leg and your left leg from the outside under his right leg in such wise that both your legs are coiled round his extremities. (Fig. 66 (E).) Your upper body is carried forward somewhat so as to effect the maximum contact between your own and your opponent's chest and abdomen. In this position while keeping your body soft and supple you contrive to control your opponent's freedom of movement and so prevent him from rising. Should he try to get up whether to right or left you must strive to foil his efforts by opening your legs coiled round his. If he discontinues his efforts you revert to your original hold-down position or by maintaining contact with your legs stretched outwards control your opponent's freedom of action. Certain variants or modifications of hand-hold (Henka) are permissible. Thus your left hand may be passed as before under your opponent's right armpit, but this time your right hand, instead of being passed under his left armpit is passed over his left-side neck. In that case your left hand takes hold of his back collar with your four fingers inside; your right hand takes a similar hold. Or else both your hands may be joined in a firm grip. Or else with your left hand you can grip your opponent's back collar and with your right hand your own left cuff. Or again you can grasp either his right and left front collar. You can also enfold your opponent's neck with both arms.

If your opponent's right arm should inadvertently become sandwiched between your right shoulder and his right-side neck, an opening may be afforded you for swift application of a modification of the Katagatame or Shoulder Lock. In that case with your right hand (which enfolds your opponent's neck from his left) you grip your own left lapel with the four fingers inside and with your left hand your right sleeve at the elbow and strongly constrict both arms.

On the principle of Kenyoho or combination methods the Tateshihogatame can sometimes be converted into a Shimewaza or Chokelock. The *modus operandi* is then as follows : With your left hand you seize your opponent's left-side collar, thumb inside, and apply your forearm to his throat. Your right arm is passed from his left-side neck to his back neck with a thrusting sensation and grips your judogi at the left elbow and in this position you may be able to subject your opponent's throat to crushing pressure from front and back.

Another quite effective version of the Tateshihogatame is described by Kudo Shihan in his useful little handbook on Judo. As before your opponent must be supine on the mat and you overlap him from the chest to the abdominal region. In quite marked contradistinction to the basic method above described you pass your *left* hand over your opponent's *left* shoulder far enough to grasp his rear belt with the thumb inside, and pull on it. Next your right hand is inserted from under his left armpit and under his left upper arm so as to stretch his arm upwards and bring the inner side of his wrist against the region of your right shoulder and with your right hand you take hold of your own left-front collar, thumb inside. Both your legs are held so high that they can be applied to the region of your opponent's armpits. Your upper body is then launched so far forward that it is prostrated obliquely over your opponent's left shoulder and the left surface of your face comes in contact with the mat. The knack of manipulating your legs in this method must be mastered to ensure its efficacy. Thus the sides of both your feet must clip your opponent's torso. (Fig. 66 (F).)

It may be useful to supplement this method with Tsunetani Oda's description of the Kuzure-Tateshihogᴀtame or Broken Lengthwise Locking of the Four Quarters. In this method your opponent must as before be lying on his back and you have assumed the astride position on his torso from his chest to his abdominal region. Your left hand is passed from over his left shoulder to his back so as to grasp his belt approximately between his middle back and his right side. Your right hand is passed from under his left armpit and upper arm to enable you to grip your own front collar. Your right elbow is tightened so that your opponent's left arm is even exposed to the risk of an Udegatame or Armlock. Your left leg is posed in such wise that from his right-side neck it is bent to enable you to squat on it with a thrusting sensation. Your right leg from his left-side abdomen thrusts into his back. Your buttocks are raised and your left-side chest is lowered. Your body in relation to your opponent assumes a leftward oblique posture. Both your feet tend to be inserted somewhat under his trunk. In this position you may be able to control his upper body and left arm. (Fig. 66 (G).)

Defence (Fusegi) or Escape Methods (Nogare-kata)

This method applies more especially to the basic version of the Tateshihogatame. Using your left hand try to unloosen your opponent's leg hold and if successful scissor his right leg between both your legs. Insert your left hand from between your opponent's right leg and your own body. Twist your body to the right. With your left hand push and lift him to the back of your right shoulder and simultaneously twist your right arm to the inside and extricate it. There are several other variants of this highly important immobilization for an exposition of which the reader is referred to my *Judo on the Ground*.

INSTRUCTION VII

ALL Japanese authorities on Shimewaza are agreed that on no account should the assailant's strangling arm be applied to his victim's throat in the semblance of an unyielding stick. It ought rather to be coiled round his neck like a clinging rope or cord which constricts an area of the victim's throat or neck very little beyond the bounds necessary to cut off his respiration. But the moment before applying the lock you are advised to take a deep breath in order to infuse the maximum strength into your body generally and your lower abdomen or saika tanden more especially. When applying the lock you must effect adequate control over your opponent so that while his balance is broken you preserve your own stability. You must practise so that you will be able to apply both hands to the most vulnerable spot on your opponent's throat. On the other hand, when you in your turn are subjected to a chokelock and realize that your respiration is in jeopardy, you are advised if still articulate to exclaim "Maitta!" ("I'm beaten!") or if deprived of speech to tap your assailant's body sharply whereupon he must at once discontinue pressure on your throat. In neither Randori nor Shiai ought Shimewaza to be attempted unless there is a Yudansha present competent in case of need to resort to Katsu or methods of resuscitation.

If you have gained reasonable proficiency in the Osaekomi-waza or hold-downs, you should be ready to tackle the more dangerous and important methods of choking and strangling an opponent into submission, whether in play or earnest. I shall try to explain the more effective chokelocks in their orthodox sequence, but it goes without saying that in either friendly competition or in a real fight you would on the spur of the moment choose the most appropriate method. The first chokelock on my list is

Namijujijime (Normal Cross)

Although chokelocks can, under certain conditions, be applied against a standing opponent from a standing position, most of them have been elaborated on the assumption that both

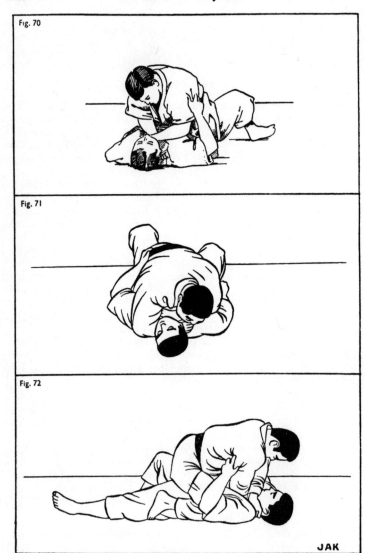

Fig. 70

Fig. 71

Fig. 72

JAK

assailant and victim will be in a more or less recumbent position or that such chokelocks will be applied from behind a seated victim by an assailant usually with one knee on the mat.

To apply the Namijujijime you sit astride your opponent's abdominal region with your knees braced on the mat at either side. With your left hand directed to your opponent's left you take a firm normal grip of his collar from behind, then cross your right arm over your left to take a similar hold of his right back collar. Remember that the normal or regular grip means that your hands are held with backs uppermost and palms downwards so that the little finger edge of your wrists constricts your opponent's neck. As you bend over him draw your arms with a sustained fluid movement to left and right and simultaneously spread your elbows outwards. Thus the efficacy of the chokelock at this final stage depends less upon the strength of your arms than upon the outward movement of your elbows. Needless to add, the potency of every Judo technique without exception gains greatly from a well-developed saika tanden or shitahara (lower abdomen), as explained in my introductory remarks. Care must ever be taken not to localize the motive power of your Tsukuri and Kake but to call into play all your bodily resources when your attack is being pressed home. (Fig. 70).

Defence : Try to insert your fingers inside your collar and by strongly pulling on it on either side endeavour to weaken the pressure on your throat. Or perhaps a sudden powerful upward push with your hand against the elbow of your assailant's uppermost arm may disturb his astride position on your stomach and capsize him to the mat on that side. Co-ordinate these manœuvres with the violent oscillation of your torso from side to side so as to weaken your assailant's astride position on your body. Speed is imperative if your defence efforts are to succeed because once your assailant's hold on your neck and throat passes a certain stage there is always danger lest sudden insensibility should supervene. So be doubly careful if you are practising these holds in the absence of a black belt competent to apply Katsu in an emergency !

Katajujijime (*Half Cross Lock*)

In this chokelock you use one hand—which is optional and immaterial—in exactly the same way as in the Namijujijime, described above, to hold your opponent's back collar in the

normal grip, i.e. with palm downward, but with the other hand
you take the so-called reverse (gyaku) grip of your opponent's
back collar, i.e. in such wise that the palm is held uppermost
so that the *thumb edge* of your wrist presses against the side of
your opponent's neck. It is, as I have said, immaterial which
hand takes the normal and which the reverse grip, but see that
the hand passing *over* your other hand takes the *normal* grip.
The hand taking the reverse grip should as much as possible
encircle the lower part of your opponent's neck. The rest of the
chokelock, Tsukuri and Kake is effected in much the same way
as in the Namijujijime. (Fig. 71).

The defence against this chokelock is similar to that against
the Namijujijime.

Gyakujujijime (Reverse Cross Lock)

To my mind this is by far the most effective of the chokelocks applied from the front with the help of the victim's
collar or lapel. In this method both your crossed hands take
the reverse hold of your opponent's back collar, i.e. your palms
are uppermost and the thumb edges of both wrists press against
your opponent's neck. For the rest the movement of your arms
at the moment of Kake necessitating the outward spreading of
your elbows resembles that of the other two chokelocks already
described.

There is, however, an additional movement calculated to
increase appreciably the efficacy of the reverse cross lock. If,
let us assume, your right hand and wrist are on top of your left,
abandon your body to your *right* and as with the momentum of
your roll you draw your opponent almost over you, encircle his
waist with your legs and interlock your feet behind his back in
the process. If, on the contrary, you roll over to your left when
your right hand and wrist are uppermost, the movement will inevitably loosen the tension of your grip and so nullify the lock.
It is naturally immaterial which of your hands is uppermost,
but when you are executing this lateral roll it is essential that
you should do so outward to the right from the thumb-edge side
of the uppermost hand if that hand is your right and to the left
when your left hand is uppermost. (Fig. 72).

The defence against this chokelock is to all intents and purposes the same as in the two preceding instances but owing to
the intrinsically greater power of the reverse cross lock the task
of escape from it is proportionally more difficult.

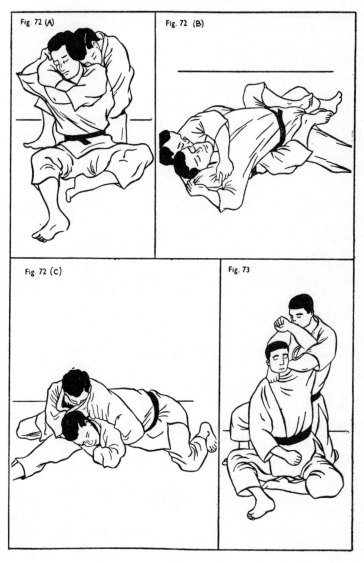

Fig. 72 (A)

Fig. 72 (B)

Fig. 72 (C)

Fig. 73

Okurierijime (Sliding Collar Lock)

We now come to a method of choking which presupposes that your opponent is seated on the mat and that you are attacking him from behind. Place your left knee on the mat. Pass your right arm over his right shoulder and across his throat and as far back as possible take a normal hold of his left lapel. Now thrust your left hand and arm under his left armpit and seize his right front lapel in the same normal grip. Place the right side of your head against the left side of your opponent's, pull his body slightly backwards and choke him with your right forearm. If your opponent tries to escape by shifting his body, since your right hand has a far-reaching hold on his left front collar, the attempt will only increase the pressure on his throat. This chokelock differs from the earlier ones described in that instead of strangulation being caused by pressure on the victim's jugular vein and carotid artery it is due to pressure on his windpipe. (Fig. 72 (A).)

It may be added that the hold with both your hands ought to be taken as deeply as possible and close contact effected between your chest and your opponent's back. At the moment of choking your opponent both your elbows should be drawn in closely to your flanks. The efficacy of the Okurierijime can often be intensified by your falling backwards, pulling your opponent with you and coiling both your legs round his body as shown in Fig. 72 (B). The object of this manoeuvre is still further to immobilize your opponent and render him more vulnerable to this particular chokelock.

Yet another quite effective variant of the Okurierijime is described as follows : In this case it is assumed that your opponent is either in a half-sitting half-rising posture or on all-fours on the mat. You approach him from his right side and from over his right shoulder pass your right hand under his throat and seize his left-side collar with your thumb inside. Your left hand is passed over the nape of his neck and inserted from under his left armpit so as to take a similar grip of his right-side collar. Then as you pull your opponent's body in the direction of his right-front corner you apply your left waist to the region of his right-side neck; both your legs assume a pose similar to that of a left Kesagatame or Scarf Holding and from this point you must exercise the weight of your body to the maximum extent and with the powerful traction of your hands consummate the chokelock. It is important that when you pull

Fig. 73(A)

Fig 74

Fig 75

your opponent's body towards his right-front corner control should not be relaxed up to the moment of strangulation. (Fig. 72 (C).)

It goes without saying that the best means of defence is to escape before your opponent has achieved complete control over your body, but failing that you should endeavour to nullify the potency of your opponent's strangling right arm by pulling strongly on it with both your hands. Switch your body to the right and try to extricate your head.

Another method : Try to pull down your opponent's right arm, then stretch your body backwards and endeavour to withdraw your head from between your opponent's right arm and breast.

Katahajime (Single Wing Lock)

In this chokelock also your opponent is supposed to be squatting or seated on the mat and you are behind him with your left knee on the ground. If you plan to choke your man with your right hand, then from your rear position pass that hand round the right side of his neck to his front and take a normal grip of his left lapel as far back as possible. Thrust your left hand and arm under his left armpit and over his left shoulder and apply the palm of the hand to the upper part of the nape of his neck, stretch your waist, pull strongly with your right hand holding his left lapel and with your left hand push his head well forward, and with this combined action choke him into submission. As a variant you can grasp your right upper forearm with your left hand and as before exert strong forward pressure against your opponent's head. (Fig. 73).

To lessen the likelihood of your opponent's escape from this necklock it is well to unbalance him backwards and to maintain the closest contact between his back and your chest. Naturally these movements should be coincident.

Defence : Before your opponent has completely thrust his hand and arm behind the nape of your neck with your right hand take hold of his right sleeve and pull it downwards against your chest, when you may perhaps succeed in foiling the attempted chokelock and escape.

Sodeguruma (Sleeve Wheel)

From the same kneeling position behind your seated opponent pass your *left* hand over his *right* shoulder and across his throat until you can take a normal grip of his *left* front collar; then pass your *right* hand across your *left* wrist and over his *left* shoulder and take hold of the slack of his tunic slightly above your *left* hand which is gripping his *left* collar. Use both hands to pull your opponent backwards and he will be speedily throttled into submission. This is one of the more effective chokelocks not usually illustrated. And in this method too the object of attack is your victim's windpipe. (Fig. 73 (A).)

Defence : Seize the left front of your collar with both hands just below your opponent's left hand and pull it down alongside the breast.

Hadakajime (*Naked Chokelock*) No. *1*

Unlike the chokelocks hitherto described, the naked chokelocks can be applied without utilizing your opponent's tunic at all, and for that reason they have a good deal to recommend them. In the first method I want to explain you make your attack from behind your opponent with your left knee on the mat. Now with the inner side of your right forearm, i.e. the thumb edge, encircle your opponent's neck from his right side so that it touches the lower part of his throat and being extended over his left shoulder enables you to place the palm of your right hand in the crook of your left elbow. To effect Kake or the final attack you should simultaneously press his head forward with your left hand applied from behind and constrict his throat with your right wrist with a combined pressing and pulling action, the latter being against your left inner arm. (Fig. 74).

Once this naked chokelock has been applied escape from it is by no means easy. Try to pull down your opponent's right forearm near the middle and draw your loins backwards so as to place your body beneath his body. If these moves succeed you may succeed in extricating yourself from your assailant's hold.

Hadakajime (*Naked Chokelock*) No. *2*

Perhaps an even simpler yet equally effective naked chokelock is the following : As before take up a semi-kneeling posture behind your opponent. Pass your left hand and arm over his left shoulder and across his throat in front with the thumb edge of your wrist against it and cup the palm of that hand in the upturned palm of your right hand near his right shoulder. Then with the left side of your head press strongly against the right side of his head and simultaneously pull hard with your right hand clasping your left so that the sustained twofold pressure on his windpipe and against his head speedily reduces him to submission.

If you prefer it you can reverse the order and instead of passing your left arm over your opponent's left shoulder pass your right arm over your opponent's right shoulder, thumb edge of wrist against his throat as before and similarly cup your right downward palm in the upturned palm of your left hand. But now the right side of your head should be pressed strongly against the 'eft side of your opponent's head.

Seeing that the efficacy of this form of Hadakajime largely depends upon the traction power of the pulling arm and that most men are stronger in their right than in their left arm, the first described method will probably prove the more popular.

You can apply a very formidable variation of the naked chokelock from behind your seated opponent while you yourself are standing up instead of kneeling. To do this you should, if using your left arm to encircle your victim's throat, place your left knee against his left shoulder, your right leg stretched conveniently to the rear and proceed as above, the left side of your head pressing firmly against the right side of his. Instead of cupping your left downward palm in your right upturned palm, you can with much the same effect clasp the back of your left hand with your overlapping right hand and so choke your victim by sustained pressure of your left wrist bone on his windpipe.

Again, as in the case of the two kneeling naked chokelocks already described, you can, if you prefer it, use your right arm to encircle your opponent's neck from behind when, of course, your right knee should be placed against your victim's right shoulder, your left leg stretched to the rear, your right cheek pressed against his left cheek, and the back of your right hand clasped tightly with your overlapping left hand. (Not illustrated).

I shall later in a separate lesson supplement my explanations of what may perhaps be regarded as the more orthodox "tricks" with a description of some others to include certain methods which, on account of their ruthlessness, have been banned in ordinary Judo competitions but methods which might conceivably serve a useful purpose in a life and death struggle.

INSTRUCTION VIII

KANSETSUWAZA OR THE ART OF BENDING AND TWISTING THE JOINTS

In this lesson there will be included several locks applied also from a standing position against a standing opponent, although most of those described presuppose that you have either yourself thrown your opponent or have caught him unawares in a more or less recumbent posture.

But before describing selected methods I intend to say a few words in explanation of an important yet simple basic principle governing the Jujutsu and Judo technique of bending and twisting the joints. On the most plausible assumption that as a rule you would be confronted by a standing opponent and that you planned to assault one of his joints, what would be your most readily accessible objective? What but one of his hands? For that reason the Jujutsu and Judo pupil is taught how most effectively to apply the basic holds against the hand of a willing subject who in his turn practises these holds on him.

Face your partner and in the first place seize his right hand from the back with both your hands in such a way that their little finger edges are laid across the base of his hand below the palm and your two thumbs are pressed against the back of his hand approximately midway between the first and second phalanges, i.e. between the first and second fingers. Exerting abdominal force try first a simple direct bending backwards of the captured hand from the wrist. It goes without saying that in a genuine attack success would almost entirely depend upon its unexpectedness. Given even the slightest warning of your intention, any man of average strength could thwart it. But a little practice in this method will suffice to convince you that it really is about the most effective that could be devised for bending your victim's hand backwards and inflicting pain on his wrist.

The next stage in the process is for you to twist the captured hand outwards and downwards to your left and your victim's

137

right, synchronizing this move with a step backwards with your left foot. This reverse action or gyaku is capable of inflicting considerable pain upon your victim and when expertly applied may even destroy his balance to his right back corner and throw him to the ground.

A corresponding hold can naturally be directed against your partner's left hand in which case the outward and downward twist should be made to your own right and your victim's left.

A hardly less painful and effective attack can be made by twisting your victim's hand outwards and *upwards* to your left and his right. If in earnest your best plan would be to seize with your right hand your victim's right hand when it happened to be hanging down rather loosely with the back turned outwards, and an instant later apply your left hand so that both your thumbs could be pressed against it between the first and second phalanges. If this outward and upward twist succeeds, your victim will usually be forced to bend forward in acute discomfort, and were you so minded you could easily convert the hold into a hammerlock beloved of " catch " tactics. The corresponding attack upon your victim's left hand necessitates a preliminary left hand hold on his wrist, supplemented by your right, then the pressure between the phalanges with both your thumbs as you twist the captured hand outwards and upwards to your right and your victim's left. If and when the last-named twist is applied and you are bent upon knocking out a real enemy, you can couple the twist with a swift kick in your victim's solar plexus delivered with your right or left foot, whichever seems more convenient. An attack of this nature would entitle it to be called a demonstration of Atemi-waza or the art of assaulting vital spots which I shall explain briefly in my tenth and last lesson of this series.

I must also point out that the Kansetsu methods described in this lesson, although fairly comprehensive in their scope, do not pretend to exhaust the Judo repertoire under this head. But an attempt to include the many subtle variations which are determined by the movements of your opponent would expand this course considerably beyond the limits set for it. For the rest, once you have mastered the basic principles, you ought to be capable yourself of improvising other locks adapted to the particular situation.

The first method I shall try to describe is called

Udegarami (Entangled Armlock)

Since disablement of your opponent's *right* arm would usually in a genuine fight prove more crippling to him than the disablement of his left arm, and since in order to achieve this laudable object you must in this particular method attack from your opponent's *left* side, on this occasion I shall assume that you are involved with your opponent in groundwork and have been manœuvring with a hold-down in view.

If, for example, you have been contemplating a Kesagatame or Scarf Hold on your opponent and are reaching over with your left arm to pass it under his right upper arm in order to grasp his right shoulder, he may in an attempt to ward off this attack push against your throat or try to grip your lapel. In that case, leaning over his torso with your right hand take hold of his right wrist in an overlapping grip, his arm being bent at the elbow; then thrust your left forearm under his right upper arm and grasp your own right wrist with your left hand also in an overlapping grip, i.e. back of hand uppermost. Now if with your right hand you continuously press your opponent's forearm downwards and with your left forearm prise up his upper arm from underneath, this remorseless counter-action will inflict severe pain on his elbow joint and if not relaxed in time will dislocate it. (Fig. 75).

If you are attacking from your opponent's *right* side, then his *left* arm must necessarily be your objective. You must then hold his left wrist with your left hand and pass your right forearm underneath his upper arm to grasp your own left wrist. Then downward pressure is exerted with your left hand on his forearm and upward pressure with your right forearm from underneath his upper arm.

If your opponent can forestall your attack by straightening his menaced arm in time, this armlock is not likely to succeed.

Udegatame or Udehishigi (Armlock or Arm Crush)

This method is best applied from either side of your opponent who is assumed to be lying on his back, and your most convenient posture for attack is one in which you have one knee on the mat.

In this case I shall assume that you are on your opponent's right side. An opportunity for attempting the Udegatame may occur if your opponent happens to stretch out his left arm to grip your right lapel or extends it near your

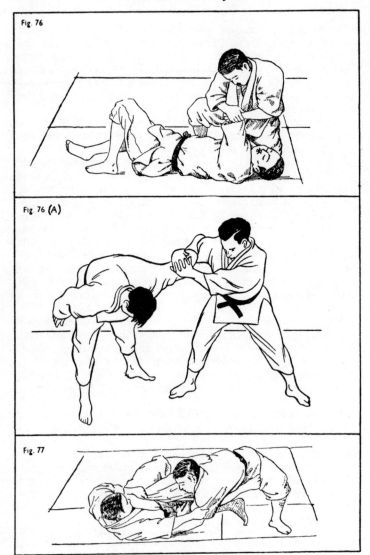

Fig. 76

Fig. 76 (A)

Fig. 77

throat. With lightning swiftness apply both hands against his left elbow joint from the outside in such wise that your left hand, palm undermost, rests directly on the joint and your right hand clasped over the back of your left hand strengthens the downward pressure in the direction of your body. Thus your opponent's arm is held in a straight line. While his elbow joint is being pushed in your direction his shoulder too cannot move and his hand is immobilized against your shoulder so that if you increase the downward pressure with both your hands on his elbow you can eventually dislocate the joint. (Fig. 76).

The following effective variant of the Udegatame is described in Kudo Shihan's little manual on the art: In this case it is assumed that you are engaged with your opponent in the Left Self-Defensive Posture or Hidarijigotai. If your opponent chances to be tightly holding your right inner upper sleeve with his left hand an opportunity may be afforded for recourse to this method. Draw your right shoulder to the rear and thereby causing your opponent to project his left shoulder simultaneously wind your right arm from the inner to the outer side of his left arm and from his left shoulder pull it downwards. This movement should coincide with the overlapping of the fingers of both your hands against his left elbow-joint, more precisely with your left palm superimposed upon the back of your right hand. Then as you swerve your body to the left you twist your opponent's elbow downwards to the utmost extent. If your opponent rotating to the front tries to escape quickly apply your left foot to the region of his right-front waist, abandon your body to the rear and instantly consummate the lock. (Fig. 76 (A).)

Defence: Should you be subjected to this form of attack the best method of escape, if you have time, is to relinquish your left-hand hold on your opponent's judogi and so separate from him.

Ude-kake-hiza-gatame (Knee Armlock)

This is a more spectacular and potentially violent and crippling lock than the two preceding ones. An opening for recourse to it may occur if while engaged in Tachiwaza or upright practice you fail to bring off a Tomoenage or Stomach Throw. Say in trying to execute this throw you have fallen on your back and your opponent has been pulled downwards in such a position that his right knee is between your thighs on the mat, his outstretched right hand touches the region of your left waist, and the outside of his elbow the inside of your left knee. At this juncture take hold of both your opponent's lower sleeves and pull him towards you. Thrust your right foot into the upper part of his left thigh or groin pushing it back so that he cannot move his body freely. Immobilize your opponent's right arm by pinning it against your left side. His right shoulder is similarly prevented from moving freely. Now press down strongly with your left knee upon his right elbow joint, your left foot and shin resting on the upper part of his right back. If your opponent doesn't give the signal of defeat in time the elbow may be dislocated. (Fig. 77).

The same lock can be equally well applied to your opponent's left elbow, should he in the midst of falling inadvertently extend his left knee between your thighs, with his outstretched left hand touching the region of your right waist and the outside of his elbow the inside of your right knee. Holding both his lower sleeves pull him as before towards you, thrust your *left* foot against his inner right thigh or groin and push it back to the fullest extent. Immobilize his left hand and arm against your right side and bring the maximum pressure of your right knee to bear upon the outside of his left elbow. Your right foot and shin are placed upon his left back.

For the success of this armlock it is of course essential that your opponent's attacked arm should be pinned with the outside of the elbow uppermost, as described above.

Defence : It should be emphasized that once these armlocks have reached a certain stage escape is bound to be difficult. However, in this case it is possible that you may be able to twist your right wrist inwards and extricate it from your opponent's left-hand hold or at any rate neutralize the lock or again you may manage to thrust it inwards in the reverse direction so that it comes into close contact with your opponent's body thus foiling the attempt.

Ashigarami (Entangled Leglock)

This is another potentially crippling lock which should never be recklessly applied save in a serious encounter with a lawless adversary bent on mischief. In much the same way as in the case of the preceding lock, an opening for the Ashigarami can occur if you have either failed to score a stomach throw with your left leg or you have deliberately missed it in order to manœuvre your adversary into a posture appropriate for recourse to the Ashigarami. Thus your opponent's left leg may be advanced towards the region of the right side of your waist. Now let go the hold of your left hand on his right sleeve and grasp his right front collar in the normal grip. Coil, as it were, your right leg round your opponent's left leg in such a way that it passes from the outside and over it until your heel comes into contact with his inner left thigh or groin. In much the same way as in the preceding lock, thrust your left foot against the inside of your opponent's right thigh or groin. Pull with both hands and push with both your feet. Your opponent's left ankle being held against your right side near your right armpit and his torso being pulled with both your hands, he cannot draw back. As your right leg from above presses down upon your opponent's left knee joint, severe pain can be inflicted and, failing submission, dislocation is likely to result. (Fig. 78).

According to circumstances the Ashigarami can be applied with equal effect to your opponent's right leg. If, for example, he exposes it to your attack by advancing it towards the region of the left side of your waist. In that case, simply as before exchange your sleeve hold for a collar or lapel hold so that both your hands are grasping his right and left lapels. Coil your *left* leg round your opponent's *right* leg from the outside and over it so that your left heel is dug into his inner right thigh or groin. Then thrust your *right* foot against the inside of your opponent's *left* thigh to help immobilize him and prevent his withdrawal. His right ankle is held against your *left* side near the armpit. Your left leg from above presses down upon your opponent's right knee joint and if your technique has been correct pain and possible dislocation will surely extort submission.

There is a minor variant in the manner of holding your opponent's collar or lapel which can also be recommended. Thus when applying the Ashigarami against your opponent's *left* leg—the method first described—you exchange your left-hand hold on your opponent's *right* sleeve in the normal grip for a reverse or gyaku grip with that hand on his *left* front collar or lapel. This means that your fingers will be inside and your thumb outside his lapel. Your right hand may hold the same lapel slightly below your left hand and in the normal grip. This method too is very powerful in its effect.

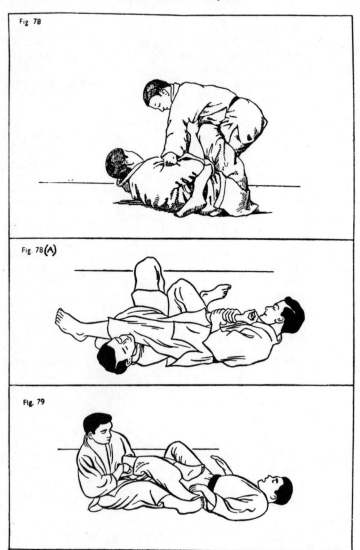

Fig 78

Fig. 78(A)

Fig. 79

Jumonjigatame or Udehishigi-juji (Cross Armlock)

I rate this as one of the more formidable Kansetsuwaza or Bonelocks. An opportunity to apply it may occur when, if you have thrown your opponent and are seated astride of him, in struggling to extricate himself or for any other reason he stretches out his right hand in an attempt to clutch your lapel. On the instant capture his right arm with both your hands and swiftly shift your position from astride of him to a seated posture at his right side as nearly as possible at right angles with his torso. The hold with your right hand should be on his wrist whereas the hold with your left hand should be somewhat further up his forearm. Naturally your right-hand grip will be from your right to left overlapping your opponent's wrist while your left-hand grip will be from left to right overlapping his forearm, and in both cases the outside edges of your little fingers will be facing his elbow. As you roll backwards from this position draw your opponent's captured right hand towards you until you have it snugly trapped in your right crotch. Extend your left leg and place it over his throat and chest to prevent him from rising. Keep your right leg bent with knee upwards and front part of the ankle in close contact with your opponent's right armpit. As you fall back be careful that your opponent's captured right arm is held with the inner side uppermost. Draw it a little towards your right side. A slight lift of your buttocks coupled with downward pressure on your opponent's arm will inflict severe pain on, and ultimate dislocation or sprain of the elbow joint unless submission comes in good time.

In the execution of this hold you must on no account lose close contact between your two bodies, and it is essential that your thigh should be kept as near as possible to the point of your opponent's shoulder—in this case the right. (Fig. 78 (A).)

Defence : With your left hand loosen your opponent's left leg, which is extended across your throat, in the direction of your head and so perhaps escape. Or else switch your body to your right, twist your trapped arm inwards and so perhaps nullify the lock.

Ashihishigi (Leglock or Leg Crush)

This is another very formidable lock which, on account of its dangerous possibilities, has been excluded from friendly club competitions. For my own part, however, I am unable to agree that it is actually more dangerous than several other methods permitted in such competitions including certain standing throws which, if clumsily executed, may easily disable the victim. In any case, considering the possible usefulness of the Ashihishigi in a real fight I feel fully justified in describing it for your benefit but with the proviso that you will never recklessly apply it in friendly practice or competition with a Judo partner.

This painful lock can be applied against a supine adversary from either your own recumbent or standing position. Once you have grasped the technique of the recumbent lock you should experience no difficulty in converting it into one applied from a standing position. Furthermore, as in virtually all Judo methods the Ashihishigi can be used against either the right or left leg of your opponent. The following is an explanation of how the lock is applied when both of you are recumbent on the mat and when you are attacking your victim's right leg.

The necessary posture for Tsukuri is one in which, usually in the course of groundwork, you are seated on the mat near your opponent's feet, say at his right side facing him. Trap your victim's right foot under your right armpit with your right arm coiled round that leg well below the knee from the inside, taking care to keep the thumb edge of your wrist-bone cutting into the flesh immediately at the base of the calf—the most sensitive spot. Your left hand may then either grip the fingers of your right hand or vice versa, whichever you prefer or you can torture your victim's right leg in a sort of bracket hold, i.e. your left hand grasps his right leg from its outside below the knee in an overlapping grip while your right hand wound under his leg in the manner already described grasps your left wrist in an overlapping grip. Synchronizing the movement with your hand hold, you must thrust your straightened right foot into your victim's left or right crotch to keep him from getting up and then while falling backwards exert the maximum upward crushing pressure against the base of the calf of the captured right leg. In a real fight this lock, if maintained for any length of time without relaxation, would effectually cripple your antagonist.

Making the necessary readjustments you can, of course, apply the Ashihishigi to your opponent's left leg. This change necessitates a preliminary posture outside your opponent's left leg and facing him as before. Pin his left leg below the knee under your left armpit with the thumb edge of your left wrist-bone digging into the flesh at the base of the calf. Decide for yourself which of the two hand-grips you prefer. If you choose the bracket hold, then your *right* hand must overlap your opponent's left leg below the knee from the outside of his leg, and your *left* hand must take an overlapping grip of your own *right* wrist. Your *left* foot must then be pushed into your opponent's left crotch to immobilize him. Kake or final attack is the same in both cases. (Fig. 79 illustrates the former variant).

The Ashihishigi can on occasion also be successfully applied from the *inside* of either the right or left leg of your opponent and with either the simple or bracket grip. But in such case you must trap his right leg under your *left* armpit and his left leg under your *right* armpit. Quite clearly, from the inside position you could not apply the crush in any other way. On the whole, however, I am inclined to think that the method first described is the more effective.

The Ashihishigi can further, as mentioned at the outset, be usefully applied by standing against a supine opponent. The several hand holds are identical with those used in a recumbent posture, but the final Kake is achieved without your having to fall on the mat. Instead it generally suffices for you to bend backwards and press strongly upwards with your thumb-edge wrist-bone crushing your victim's lower calf, as already described.

Udehijigi (Arm Bracket) or Udehishigi (Arm Crush)

This is a lock to be attempted when both you and your opponent are engaged in a standing position. An opening for its application can occur if your opponent carelessly stretches his right arm to his front. With your right hand grasp his right wrist from its inner side so that the thumb side points towards his elbow, and the inner side of his arm is kept uppermost, i.e. your hand must be over his wrist. Advance your left foot a little and turn your body to the right so as to bring you round to his right side. Pin your opponent's right upper arm under your left armpit. Your left under arm should be held in close contact with your opponent's elbow or its upper part and should pass underneath so that with your left hand you can grasp your own right lower lapel. The rôle of your right hand gripping your opponent's right wrist is to push the latter downwards in the

Fig. 80

Fig. 81

reverse direction, forcing your opponent to tilt forward on his toes. As you keep up the downward pressure on his right wrist he is unable to relax and severe pain is inflicted on his elbow joint culminating in dislocation if he does not surrender. For the successful execution of this lock it is essential that while pressing your opponent's wrist downwards its inner side is uninterruptedly kept turned upwards. Should he manage to loosen it, the efficacy of the lock will be lost. (Fig. 80).

This lock can equally well be applied against your opponent's left arm, should he afford you an opening by carelessly stretching it to his front. You should by this time be able to work out the necessary modifications for yourself. Your left hand must now grasp his left inner wrist from above and the encircling arm is your right, with your opponent's left upper arm pinned under your own right armpit, and the hand of your encircling arm holding your own left lower lapel or thereabouts. You have naturally swerved round to your opponent's left side. The successive steps to the final Kake are much the same.

Udehishigi-wakigatame (Side Arm Crush or Lock)

This somewhat awkwardly designated lock might be essayed by you against an assailant who had grasped your throat from the front with both hands intending to throttle you. Take hold of his right wrist from the outside with your left hand and of his hand from the inside with your right hand in proximity. Keep your body straight but leaning back slightly and co-ordinate this move with a powerful well-sustained inward twist (to your own right) on your opponent's captured right arm. As you do this pivot more to your right and bring your opponent's arm underneath your left armpit with your left arm pressed firmly against his elbow joint from the outside. At this stage bend backwards and try to combine your downward pressure of your arm against your victim's elbow joint with a backward bend of his wrist with your hands, thus threatening him with a dual dislocation or painful sprain. In all cases when applying these locks try to call into play the latent power of your saika tanden or lower abdomen and not to confine your effort solely to your arms and/or legs. (Fig. 81).

If you are applying this arm crush to your opponent's left arm to counter his attempt to choke you from the front, then your right hand takes the outer grip of his wrist and your left hand the inner hold of his hand. The inward twist of his arm

is then to your left. Your opponent's left arm is brought under
your right armpit and you pivot to your left. The succeeding
movements are the same as in the first instance.

Arm Entanglement in Retort to attempted Blow

This particular method is not generally listed in Judo textbooks and I have never seen a precise Japanese definition.
Doubtless, however, it would figure among the Udegarami or
entangled armlocks.

Assume that your opponent has aimed a blow at your head
with his right fist. Intercept—if you can!—this blow by captur-
ing his wrist with your left hand. Violently bend his arm
upwards at the elbow and as you advance against him thread
your right forearm underneath his right upper arm and place
the palm of your hand so that it overlaps your left hand which
is gripping his wrist. Combine downward pressure with your
left hand on his wrist with an upward prising pressure of your
right arm from under his right upper arm. Keep as far to your
left and as close to your opponent as possible and turn your
head and face also well to your left in order not to expose yourself to the risk of a swinging uppercut with your opponent's
left fist on the point of your jaw. Such a fate once befell a not
very large Japanese policeman who tried to demonstrate this
particular hold on a big and powerful English friend of mine,
a hotel proprietor in the Japanese lake district. The Japanese
policeman went down for the count. So take heed how you
try this hold on a tough antagonist handy with his mits! (Not
illustrated).

Before completing this description of chosen bonelocks and
holds which does not profess to be exhaustive, I don't think I
can do better than quote some cautionary comment on the
subject volunteered to me many years ago at the Tokyo
Kodokan by the famous Judo master Sakujiro Yokoyama, now,
alas, no more, who honoured me with his friendship throughout
my membership of that school. It was to this effect, freely
translated from the original Japanese into colloquial English :

"All these fancy holds and locks are very well in their way.
But one has to be very careful how one tries them out against
a rough and tough opponent, especially if you are not quite
sure that he is wholly ignorant of Jujutsu or Judo. So when
in doubt the best plan is, in my opinion, to close with your
man right away and throw him heavily with one of the recog-

nized hand, foot, leg or hip throws. Once you have him on the ground, he is virtually at your mercy and far more amenable to Kansetsuwaza than when he is standing up."

So please bear this advice in mind when practising the standing Kansetsuwaza explained above (and equally when studying the unorthodox and irregular methods I shall do my best to describe in my next instruction).

INSTRUCTION IX

THERE is always the likelihood latent in every technical textbook that some at any rate of the methods described will
already be known to some if not all readers. This risk must be
faced, and I can but hope that readers will not be over exacting
and will not grumble should portions of these pages turn out to
be familiar. Moreover it is well to recall in this context the sage
counsel of Alexander Pope embodied in the oft quoted lines :

> " A little learning is a dangerous thing;
>   Drink deep or taste not the Pierian spring;
>   There shallow draughts intoxicate the brain,
>   And drinking largely sobers them again ".

In any case, a writer on a technical subject is bound to proceed on the assumption that his readers know next to nothing
about it and must therefore be thoroughly grounded in basic
principles before they can safely pass on to their elaboration
and practical application.

I want now to begin with a description of the simplest and
most effective manner of extricating yourself from a hand grip
put upon you perhaps by an opponent larger and stronger than
yourself and therefore confident in his ability to render you
helpless.

Instead of dissipating your energies by aimlessly tugging at
your captor's hands, note the position of his *thumbs*. If he has
taken the grip of your two wrists with his thumbs *uppermost*,
lower your waist slightly, draw in your elbows and invoking the
force of your saika tanden or lower abdomen push steadily upwards and outward to right and left. The leverage against the
assailant's thumb is so powerful that very few wrist holds from
the front, however strong the assailant may be, can resist this
breakaway.

Should your opponent have grasped your wrists with his

thumbs *below*, merely reverse the escape movement bv pressing *downwards* and outwards against them.

On the doubtful hypothesis that an attacker would be so foolish as to seize one of your wrists with both hands, thus leaving you with a free hand and arm to strike with, if you are loath to be so rough, you can use it to reinforce the upward or downward thrust of your captured hand according to the position of your attacker's thumbs. Thus if your right wrist is held and your attacker's thumbs are uppermost, insert your left hand between your assailant's two hands and use it to strengthen the leverage of your right arm.

Another plan, perhaps a better one, is to advance a step and lower your body so that your elbow is below your assailant's hands. Keep it bent at an acute angle. Making the fullest use of your weight push upwards and force your wrist out of his grasp. Remember always to supplement all these moves with your abdominal power.

The most effective breakaway from a wrist hold in which your assailant's thumbs are underneath is to turn your body slightly to your left so as to bring your right elbow vertically over your fist; then using the weight of your body and your abdominal power force your hand down through his fingers. A complementary push against his torso with your right shoulder can put him off balance and still further facilitate your breakaway.

However, if you know anything about boxing and your assailant's intentions were really unfriendly, an uppercut with your free left fist to the point of his jaw would obviate the necessity for a breakaway. And if you have assimilated the admittedly superficial instruction in Atemiwaza or the art of attacking vital spots provided in my next and last lesson in this series you could just as readily knock him out for more than the count with a slicing blow to his left carotid artery delivered with the little finger edge of your free left hand.

As in the case of the Kansetuwaza described in Instruction VIII, the foregoing wrist breakaways by no means exhaust the available supply, but I do not consider this section of the art of such vital importance as to justify further extension of the list, and once you have familiarized yourself with these breakaways you will, I think, find them sufficient to meet most contingencies likely to arise in real life.

Counter to Attempted Necklocks From the Front

Instruction VIII already includes one method, the Udehishigi-wakigatame or Side Arm Crush which can be usefully applied against such an attempted necklock. The following three simpler methods can also be recommended :

No. 1. Clasp your hands together and drive them from either left or right against your assailant's outstretched arms. This move should suffice to break his hold.

No. 2. Again clasp your hands; then suddenly thrust your arms upwards between your opponent's arms and as close to his wrists as possible. The violent separation of your arms should break his hold.

No. 3. Bring your left forearm over your opponent's right and under his left arm. Cup your left hand in your right, force your left forearm upwards and twist your opponent's arms to the left. If further punishment seems advisable, you might step in and drive your knee into your opponent's groin and perhaps couple this attack with an Atemi chop with the little finger edge of your right or left hand against his carotid artery or jugular vein. Always remember to reinforce every such attack with the weight of your body and the power emanating from your saika tanden.

No. 4. Last but not least, the Yokosutemi or Side Body Throw can be successfully invoked if you are quick enough. Hold your opponent's left lapel with your right hand and his right sleeve with your left hand. His very grip on your throat will facilitate the task of breaking his balance towards his right front corner. Abandon yourself slightly to the left as you fall. Keep your left leg just outside his right foot. Synchronize your fall with a strong upward lift with your right hand gripping your opponent's left lapel and an equally strong downward pull with your left hand holding his right sleeve. The combined impetus of your own fall and hand action should suffice both to break his incipient stranglehold and to hurl him to the mat or ground away over to your own left. If you find it inconvenient to get a left lapel hold with your right hand, try suddenly pushing up with that hand the elbow of his left arm the hand of which is gripping the right side of your neck. By forcing his left arm upwards and sideways to your left you may get him off balance and so appreciably strengthen the momentum of your " sacrifice " fall. It will be easier to raise his left elbow if his left wrist is crossed *over* his right wrist in either a normal or reverse chokelock on your throat but should it happen to be undermost you can alternatively try your Yokosutemi to your *right* side and use your *left* hand to thrust his *right* upper arm upwards from underneath his elbow. But in that case it might be advisable to substitute for your right hand hold on his left lapel a right hand hold on his left sleeve.

That I am not here merely wandering in the realm of hypothesis will appear from the fact that many years ago during a Judo lecture and demonstration given by me at the British Consul's house at Tsangkou, China, I successfully applied the Yokosutemi to foil a sudden assault on my throat made by an athletic member of my audience. He was sent flying across the mats and came to a sudden halt against a flower-pot which he shattered!

Counters to Front Waist Holds

Although only an arrant idiot or tyro would seriously encircle the waist of an able-bodied man from the front in the hope of overpowering him, still on the assumption that it takes all sorts to make a world, I had better cite a few simple methods of countering such an imbecile method of attack.

No. 1. At the moment your assailant's arms are passing round your waist, thrust your left forearm underneath his right upper arm with the thumb edge of your wrist-bone held against his arm somewhat above his elbow. With the palm of your right hand press heavily against the frontal point of his right shoulder and with your left hand clasp your right wrist from above with fingers overlapping. Apply counter action by prising up your opponent's right upper arm from beneath with your left forearm and pressing down his right shoulder from above with your right hand. Bend back slightly and bring your saika tanden into operation. The knack of this particular " entanglement " may take some little time to acquire, but if the " entanglement " is properly executed severe pain is inflicted on the victim and dislocation of the shoulder might even ensue if the hold were long enough maintained.

No. 2. A violent upward thrust with your right hand aimed at the tip of your opponent's nose, in such wise that the lower fleshy ridge of your open palm causes the impact, is calculated to disconcert most people.

No. 3. If your opponent has actually succeeded in encircling your waist and has already lifted you from the ground in con-

templation of hurling you down again, losing no time press
your right palm violently against his forehead from the tip of
his nose upwards and thrust back his head with maximum
force. The odds are that he will collapse as though poleaxed to
escape a broken neck.

I was once privileged in Japan during the Russo-Japanese
war to witness a real life demonstration of the efficacy of this
counter to a frontal waist lift. As Tokyo correspondent for the
London *Daily Mail* I was paying a visit to a prisoner-of-war
camp at Narashino near Tokyo, accompanied by a Japanese
judoka of my acquaintance, not a member of the Kodokan but
of another ryugi or school. On our arrival at the camp we
found a group of Russians engaged in an impromptu wrestling
match. The evident champion, a powerful thick-set specimen,
invited my Japanese friend to " have a go ". My friend con-
sented. Then the moment they faced each other in the arena
the Russian got his mighty arms round my friend's waist, swung
him bodily in the air and clearly concluded that all was over
save the shouting, when my friend suddenly applied the counter
described above and the Russian ignominiously bit the dust,
figuratively speaking, greatly to the surprise if not edification of
the onlookers who had confidently anticipated an easy triumph
for their champion.

Counters to Seizure from Behind

There are many of these counters but the appended selection
seems to me to include the more practical methods, firstly, to
a rear hold under your arms and secondly, to a rear hold pinning your arms to your sides.

Anybody so ill advised as to clasp your waist from behind
under your arms is simply asking for trouble since he has con-
siderately left at your disposal both your elbows which are
among the more formidable natural weapons available to the
judoka possessing even a superficial knowledge of Atemiwaza
or the art of attacking vital spots. But your first obvious retort
to this crude method of attack is to bash your assailant in the
nose with the back of your head. As in every analogous
instance, concentrate in the blow all your bodily strength from
your saika tanden upwards. As his head is jolted backwards
pivot slightly to your right and with your right elbow deal him
a violent blow on his neck or the point of his jaw. If he ducks
to his left twist your body to your left and deal him a violent

blow with your left elbow on his jaw or neck. Then if this treat-
ment induces him to stagger back a pace or two, jab him
violently in the stomach or solar plexus with either elbow and
so knock him out. Ever bear in mind the necessity of supplementing all local action with the power emanating from your
saika tanden.

If seized from behind so that your assailant has pinned your
arms to your sides, as in the foregoing instance bash him on
the nose with the back of your head or if you happen to be
much shorter than your adversary stamp hard on his instep;
then taking instant advantage of the momentary slackening of
his hold, hunch your shoulders, drop on your right knee, apply
your left hand to the front of his left thigh, grasp his right collar
with your right hand and sling him over your right shoulder
in much the same way as in the case of the Seoiotoshi described
elsewhere in Instruction II.

Another method sometimes favoured is to bend down, then
with both hands clutch your assailant's ankles, pull his legs up
between your own and as he crashes come down yourself backwards as heavily as possible upon his stomach. The double
shock is calculated to cool his ardour for a continuation of the
struggle.

Combined Trunk Squeeze and Reverse Stranglehold
    (Japanese Term : Dojime and Gyakujujijime)

Let me say at once that this method is no longer allowed in
friendly competitions for fear of injury to the victim. Yet in my
day both at the Kodokan and the Tenshin Shinyo-ryu school
which I used to attend it was practised as a matter of course,
and personally I cannot agree that it is really any more
dangerous than several other permitted methods of defence and
attack. It would certainly be admissible to counter a serious
frontal attack. It could even be invoked against an assailant
who had seized you round the waist under your arms or against
one who had closed and was grappling with you. For its success
you must first manage to apply the reverse chokelock or
stranglehold (Gyakujujijime) to your opponent's neck and
throat. I hope you haven't forgotten this. Remember that in
contradistinction to the so-called " Normal Cross Lock "
(Namijujijime), your palms are held uppermost and the thumb-
side edges of your wrist-bones constrict your victim's jugular
vein and carotid artery. Synchronize the application of this

lock with your backward fall and at the same time encircle your opponent's waist with your legs below the ribs and interlock your feet behind his back. Drag him to the ground over you and combine the maximum pressure of both your knees against both sides of his trunk with the maximum constriction of his neck and throat with your hands. Unless his powers of resistance are abnormally great he must either give in or pass out.

As I have already said, the Dojime either alone or in combination with any other method is not allowed in club competitions, but this rule need not deter you from practising it by agreement with your partner who should on no account delay giving the signal of defeat the moment he begins to experience the warning symptoms of a choking sensation, a singing in the ears and a feeling as though his eyes were popping out of their sockets. In a real fight you would not, of course, hesitate to give your opponent his quietus. You in your turn should be on the look-out for these tell-tale premonitory symptoms and, if engaged in a friendly tussle, relax your grip in good time.

By way of defence against the Dojime alone, try to dig your elbows as far down as possible between your assailant's gripping thighs and your own body and press strongly outwards with them and so compel him to relax his hold. In a real fight you need not scruple to dig your thumbs into his groins on either side thereby inflicting such pain that he will be forced to abandon the hold.

A useful method of foiling an assailant's attempt to encircle your waist from the front is the following : Grasp his belt or the top of his trousers with either hand, and with your free hand hit him hard on the point of the jaw. Follow up by pushing back his chin with the hand that delivered the blow and by pulling him with the hand holding his belt or trousers, thus hurling him to the ground.

How to Seize an Opponent From Behind

From what I have said about counters to seizure from your rear it should be obvious that the methods attempted by your assailant are incorrect.

If, therefore, the roles are reversed and you wish to bring your opponent to the ground from behind without otherwise hurting him, simply place your hands on his shoulders and jab your right or left knee into the small of his back or alternatively place your right instep behind his right knee, knock his

knee forward and pull his shoulders back. Then as he falls back
against your chest pass your arms under his armpits and lower
him to the ground. After that he ought to be entirely at your
mercy.

Leg Entanglement from Supine Position

I describe the following method for what it may be worth
but without wholeheartedly recommending it as a decisive
technique in itself.

If facing an oncoming assailant, instead of, say, attempting
to get to grips and apply the Tomoenage or Stomach Throw,
drop on your back and as soon as your attacker is within reach
hook his *left* ankle from the *outside* with the *back* of your *left*
foot; simultaneously press the sole of your *right* foot strongly
against his left knee-cap from the inside. Couple a pull with
your left foot hooking his left ankle with the press of the sole
of your right foot against his knee-cap and the odds are that
he will lose his balance and fall backwards to the ground. If so
it ought not to be very difficult for you to trap his left leg in the
Ashihishigi or Leglock described in Instruction VIII. Incidentally, if instead of merely pressing your opponent's knee-cap
with the sole of your foot you were to convert such pressure
into a violent kick, you might even dislocate his knee-cap.

This Leg Entanglement can, of course, be applied to your
adversary's right leg by reversing the movement, but as a rule
the attack on the left leg seems the more convenient.

Dangerous Necklock Counter to Scarf Hold

This is another violent counter measure wholly forbidden in
friendly competitions, but one which in my early days at the
Yokohama dojo of the Tenshin Shinyo-ryu we never scrupled
to apply.

Say you have been thrown in a sudden attack and your
assailant is bending over you from either side approximately
in a posture reminiscent of that adopted for the application of
the Kesagatame or Scarf Hold described in Instruction VI.
Assuming that he is on your left side proceed as follows : Place
your palms under his chin and shove his head violently backwards. In swift sequence bring up your right leg, place the
lower part of the calf across his throat and with all your force
thrust his head backwards towards your feet. If at the same
time you take hold of his right sleeve with your left hand

dropped from his chin, the resultant counter action may very well endanger his neck. In any case it is calculated to render him helpless and exposed to your successive attack (Renzoku-waza). If he has been bending over you from your right flank, merely change legs : your *left* leg is then brought up and passed across his throat. The final stages are the same as in the former instance.

I now append a description of four highly dangerous neck and spine locks (Kubigatame) for which I am indebted to my friend N. Livingstone-Learmonth who took the trouble to translate the details from the "Manuel Complet de Judo et Jujutsu", edited by Messrs. Lamotte and Marcelin. His description was originally printed in the October, 1950, number of the Quarterly Bulletin of the London Budo'swai from which I have copied it with due acknowledgment. In doing so I must in turn repeat his warning that these locks are extremely dangerous and should never be prartised unless under the direct supervision of a Black Belt.

Tsurijime (Pull Choke)

With your opponent lying on his back you should squat on his chest and place both hands on the back of his neck, high up towards the occiput. While applying your whole weight upon his chest press his head towards you with your hands. This hold extends the upper spinal vertebra and can be fatal.

Yokohanten (Side Turnover)

While in the prone position on your left side facing your prone opponent, encircle his waist with both legs in the scissor-hold described by me for the Dojime (Trunk Squeezing). At the same time pass your *right* arm from the rear over his *right* shoulder around the back of his neck thus bringing his head beneath your *right* armpit. A combination of both kidney-squeeze and spine lock will soon make him submit.

Kensuigatame (Hanging Choke)

A simple standing necklock. Force down your opponent's head with your left hand, slipping your right arm beneath his throat. Pass your left arm over the back of his neck. Place your right palm in the crook of your left elbow, as in the Hadaka-jime or Naked Chokelock, and press down on the top of his head with your right armpit. Now twist his neck raising him as much as possible.

Fukurokensui (Hanging Bag)

In this hold you are standing and your opponent is presumed to be lying on his back, his feet towards you. Raise his legs in the air, slipping one over each of your shoulders, and take hold of his belt with your hands. Now lean right over him, using all your weight to press down upon his neck and spine.

To my mind the third method described, the Kensuigatame or Hanging Choke, is the poorest of the four. It is fraught with the peril ever latent in all fancy holds attempted from the standing position in that any prospective victim apprised of your amiable intention, as he could hardly avoid being, could easily hit you hard in your solar plexus with his fist or jab it with his elbow before completion of the hold. An even tenderer portion of your anatomy would also be very vulnerable to attack!

INSTRUCTION X

ATEMIWAZA OR THE ART OF ATTACKING VITAL SPOTS

IT has been pointed out by the late Sakujiro Yokoyama in his classic textbook on Judo that among the older Jujutsu schools instruction was concerned chiefly with preparing the pupil for contest. For this purpose the curriculum included not only Nagewaza and Katamewaza but equally Atemiwaza or the art of attacking vital spots. Nevertheless since the last-named branch was regarded as esoteric or secret, beginners were not readily initiated into its methods. But in Yokoyama's opinion, the harm likely to result from the teaching of Atemiwaza is not sufficient to warrant its retention as a permanent mystery. On the other hand, considering that in contest the risks attendant on its application would be too great, instruction can for the most part be little more than theoretical. Generally too it is imperative that the utmost caution and circumspection should be exercised in the diffusion of this dangerous knowledge. Mindful of this responsibility, it is the rule alike at the Tokyo Kodokan and most Judo clubs in other parts of the world that instruction in Atemiwaza should be withheld until the student has attained the "Dan" or Black Belt grade, by which time he ought rightly to have developed not only physical skill but certain moral qualities calculated to deter him from the reckless abuse of his special knowledge.

Since the methods of Atemiwaza comprise not only hitting vital spots with the fist but poking with the fingers, "chopping" with the little finger edge of the hand, jabbing with the elbow, battering with the head, jolting with the knee-cap and kicking with the ball of the foot and the heel, it is clear that unlike Randori or Kata, Atemiwaza could not be safely practised with a human partner or only to a very limited extent. Use is therefore made of rolled straw, sand-bags, the punching ball or even a wooden wall so as to develop the necessary degree of accuracy and power in applying the various techniques. Lacking absolute proficiency in such methods, the tyro who relied upon Atemiwaza for victory in a genuine emergency would be courting disaster.

Atemiwaza cannot therefore be safely taught until the pupil has already become well grounded in Nagewaza (the art of throwing) and Katamewaza (groundwork) exemplified in both Randori (free exercise) and Shobu or Shiai (contest) and even in the various Kata or prearranged forms whereby he can best complete bodily tempering and control of movement.

In this lesson I make no pretence to anything like an exhaustive survey of the subject, not only because my own knowledge is far from complete but also because I do not deem it advisable to furnish too many details which, should they be widely diffused, might be prostituted to base ends by unscrupulous persons.

The wide scope of Atemiwaza will appear from some observations made by Dr. Yamada Yasushi, 7th Dan of the Kodokan, i.e.

In attacking, there are 38 methods :

With the use of the fingers	13
With the fist	10
With the ulnar border of the hand, the palm and elbow	7
With the foot	5
With the head	3

As each can be applied to right or left, this makes a total of 76, without counting the different variations in the manner of applying the blows. In striking in Atemi one must strengthen the mind and body. Occasionally when the need is great and one's life is in danger one must use whatever comes to hand in striking at the vital spots : with a glass, stick, burning brand, boiling water, etc., the most important point here being to strike only at the vital spots. Here is a list of 80 Atemi spots easily to be found on the anatomical charts in works of acupuncture :

Head	19	spots
Neck	9	spots
Chest	16	spots
Stomach	17	spots
Arm	6	spots
Leg	13	spots

The chart supplied (Fig. 82) in this section gives only ten vital spots, although I have specified twelve in the text. Very

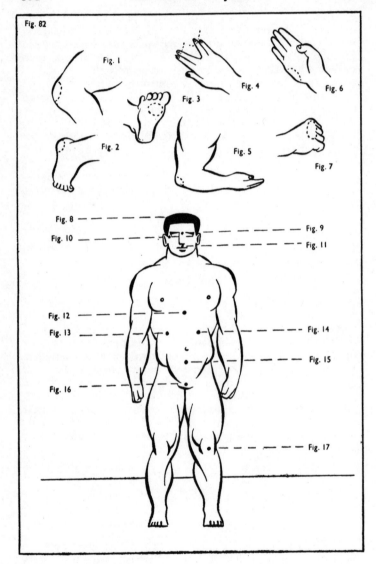

Fig. 82

few more are known to myself. None the less, a judoka familiar with these spots and thoroughly versed in the correct methods of assaulting them would be a decidedly formidable customer in unarmed combat.

A fundamental rule which must be observed if any Atemi method is to become fully effective is that after delivering the particular attack, whether with the finger end, the ulnar border of the hand, the fist, the elbow, the ball of the foot or toe, the knee-cap or the heel, you should with lightning-like rapidity bring back the attacking member to its starting-point. As Yokoyama remarks in his chapter on Atemiwaza, if you neglect this rule, even though you may have accurately struck the relevant vital spot, the efficacy of your attack will be appreciably lessened. According to circumstances, Atemiwaza can be equally well applied against either a standing or lying adversary.

The vital spots (Kyusho) enumerated below together with the respective methods of attacking them correspond to those shown on the attached chart and should be checked in relation to the latter. As I have already said, Kasumi (temples) and Kachikake (chin) are not shown on the chart. A list of the original Japanese terms is also supplied for reference. These terms generally possess the advantage of greater conciseness than their English equivalents.

Tendo (Bregma, top of head) : Perhaps the least convenient spot of all for attack without a lethal weapon.

Uto (Nasion) : Approximately the spot in the middle of the forehead. This can be hit or poked. Although the clenched fist may be used for this purpose, a blow with the little finger edge of the hand is the most effective.

Kasumi (Temples) : Not shown on chart but easily identifiable. They can be struck violently with the little finger edge of the hand. If the attack is successful the victim faints.

Dokko (Mastoid process behind the ears) : If your opponent is already on the ground and at your mercy, you can inflict great pain on him by pressing the knuckle of your second finger against this spot.

Jinchu (Philtrum) : The spot under the nose. This spot can be effectively struck with the fist, the little finger edge of the hand, or elbow. It is highly sensitive.

Kachikake (Chin) : Not shown on chart but familiar to everybody. It can be attacked with the fist or elbow.

Suigetsu (Solar Plexus or pit of the stomach) : This spot can be powerfully hit with the fist, elbow, knee-cap or can be kicked. As in boxing, so in Atemiwaza, this vital spot is one of the most vulnerable in the human body. On an Atemi chart bequeathed to me by my first Jujutsu (not Judo) teacher of the Tenshin Shinyo-ryu at Yokohama, this spot is described as the most secret of that school. When kicking your opponent in this spot, keep the toes curved and deliver the blow with the ball of the foot. Remember to withdraw the foot as also any other member used for this attack instantaneously after delivering the blow.

Denko and Getsuei (Hypochondrium) : Region of the lower ribs. It can be struck or kicked. The right side is called Denko and the left side Getsuei.

Myojo (Hypogastrium) : About an inch below the navel. It can be powerfully kicked.

Tsurigane (Testicles) : It can be assaulted with the knee-cap or finger-tips or kicked.

Shitsukansetsu (Knee-joint) : It can be kicked. A fairly effective method of attacking it is described in Instruction IX.

The relevant parts with which to attack an opponent are appended. The sequence is given to correspond approximately with the figures shown at the top of the diagram included in this section.

Fig. 1. *Hizagashira* : Patella or knee-cap.

Fig. 2. *Kakato* : Heel.

Fig. 3. *Ashiura* : The ball of the foot.

Fig. 4. *Ryogantsuki* : Middle finger and ring finger end.

Fig. 5. Olecranon or elbow.

Fig. 6. *Tsukidashi* (finger end) and *Tegatana* (ulnar border of hand).

Fig. 7. *Kobushi* (fist) and *Horyu* (the side fist).

The suffix *ate* (pronounced " ah-teh ") usually attached to the root word means to strike, thrust, poke, kick, etc., as the case may be. Thus the term " Ude-ate " means the art of attacking the vital spots with any part of the arm, and "Ashi-ate " means the art of attacking the vital spots with any part of the foot or leg. Furthermore, under the former heading we get :

Yubisakiate or attack with the finger tip.

Kobushiate or attack with the fist.

Tegatana-ate or attack with the little finger edge.

Hijiate or attack with the elbow.

Under the latter heading we get :

Hizagashira-ate or attack with the knee-cap.
Sekitoate or attack with the ball of the foot.
Kakatoate or attack with the heel.

There are also pertinent to each of these classifications many Japanese subsidiary terms descriptive of the nature of the attack, e.g., whether a blow, poke, thrust, kick, etc., delivered directly, obliquely, slantwise, from above, from the rear, etc., etc. Thus, for example, " Nanameate" implies an oblique or slanting blow, "Yokoate" a lateral blow, "Ueate" a blow from above, " Tsukiage" an upward thrust, " Shitatsuki " a downward thrust, " Ushirotsuki " a rear thrust, " Ushirosumitsuki " a rear corner thrust, " Tsukkake", straight, direct, " Uchioroshi ", a downright blow on the head. These terms are applicable to the fist. The term " kirioroshi ", applicable to the little finger edge, implies a downward slicing blow. " Maeate ", applicable to the knee-cap, means a frontal attack. "Ushiroate," applicable to the elbow, means a rear blow. In the case of the ball of the foot and the heel, we have " Maekeri " or frontal kick, " Yokokeri" or lateral kick, " Ushirokeri " or rear kick, etc. An exhaustive citation of all these subtleties would tend rather to confuse than to enlighten the reader, and has therefore been avoided.

And here I must reluctantly take leave of my readers for the time being. I do so with the repeated intimation that the methods described in all ten Instructions of this manual very far from exhaust the Judo repertoire whose name is veritably legion. In any case it is the considered opinion of nearly every experienced yudansha or holder of " Dan " rank that the mastery of comparatively few methods is always preferable to a superficial knowledge of many. Throughout my own long membership of the Kodokan I witnessed the exemplification of this truism in countless contests wherein the victors almost invariably scored with not more than two or three throws at most. Even when their opponents had been apprised beforehand of their " specialities ", they were usually caught napping.

All-time professional instructors are in a special category and must of necessity familiarize themselves with the minutiae of virtually all Judo techniques. The case is otherwise with the amateur whose main purpose in studying Judo is usually the mixed one of acquiring an art intrinsically valuable as an almost unrivalled system of unarmed defence and attack, without lethal weapons, and at the same time a splendid means of keeping its votaries physically and mentally fit.

The best parting advice I can offer you is that you should conscientiously try out all the methods described in this manual, then discard those that seem to you least suited to your physical and mental make-up and finally concentrate on the residue until at least approximate mastery has been achieved.

INDEX